GRADE
K-12

A HANDBOOK FOR TEACHERS

. . . .

Effective
Instructional Strategies

VOLUME 2

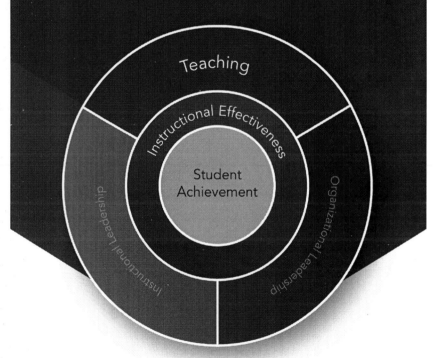

Teaching

Instructional Effectiveness

Student
Achievement

Instructional Leadership

Organizational Leadership

International Center for
Leadership in Education
Rigor, Relevance, and Relationships for ALL Students

Acknowledgments

The International Center for Leadership in Education wishes to thank
the authors of this handbook:
Richard D. Jones, Ph.D., Lead Author
Nancy Caramanico
Ellen Harris
Tammy Mose-Cooper
Amanda Orndorff
Gayle Palka
Sherry St. Clair

Published by International Center for
Leadership in Education, Inc.

Printed in the U.S.A.

ISBN-13: 978-1-935300-77-9
ISBN-10: 1-935300-77-6

International Center for Leadership in Education, Inc.
1587 Route 146
Rexford, New York 12148
(518) 399-2776
info@LeaderEd.com

090113

Contents

 **Overview**

The Daggett System for Effective Instruction

The Daggett System for Effective Instruction (DSEI) provides a coherent focus across the entire education organization on the development and support of instructional effectiveness to improve student achievement. Whereas traditional teaching frameworks are teacher-focused and consider what teachers should do to deliver instruction, DSEI is student-focused and considers what the entire educational system should do to facilitate learning. It is a subtle but important difference based on current research and understanding about teaching and learning.

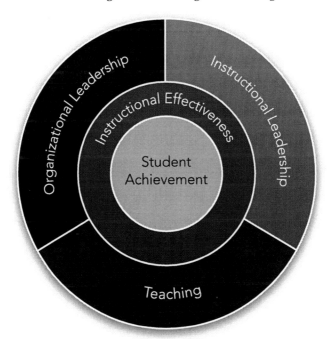

The three parts of DSEI are illustrated here. The following are the critical functions of each part of the system. Think about where you, as a professional educator, fit into this system.

Six Elements of Organizational Leadership

- Create a culture of high expectations.
- Create a shared vision.
- Build leadership capacity.
- Align organizational structures and systems to vision.
- Align teacher/administrator selection, support, and evaluation.
- Support decision making with data systems.

Five Elements of Instructional Leadership

- Use research to establish urgency for higher expectations.
- Align curriculum to standards.
- Integrate literacy and math across all content areas.
- Facilitate data-driven decision making to inform instruction.
- Provide opportunities for focused professional collaboration and growth.

Six Elements of Teaching

- Embrace rigorous and relevant expectations for all students.
- Build strong relationships with students.
- Possess depth of content knowledge and make it relevant to students.
- Facilitate rigorous and relevant instruction based on how students learn.
- Demonstrate expertise in use of instructional strategies, technology, and best practices.
- Use assessments to guide and differentiate instruction.

When all parts of the system are working together efficiently, teachers receive the support they need, and students are successfully prepared for college, careers, and citizenship.

Effective Instructional Strategies and Rigor and Relevance

This handbook is a continuation of *Effective Instructional Strategies — Volume 1.* It presents an additional 19 instructional strategies, all correlated to the Rigor/Relevance Framework® as well as to various types of assessment, to student learning styles, and to the use of technology. This handbook fits with the DSEI in the Teaching segment: demonstrate expertise in use of instructional strategies, technology and best practices; facilitate rigorous and relevant instruction based on how students learn; possess depth of content knowledge and make it relevant to students; and use assessments to guide and differentiate instruction.

Artistic Expression

This chapter discusses the role of the arts within the core curriculum and its use in improving academics. Specific examples are given on ways to integrate the arts into language arts, mathematics, science, and multiple disciplines.

Compare and Contrast

Compare and contrast promotes rigorous thinking. This chapter suggests a range of compare-and-contrast strategies suitable for different curricula.

Digital Media Production

This chapter explores the use of digital media in ways that also enable students to express themselves in traditional ways, such as writing. Three types are reviewed: digital video, podcasting and vodcasting, and blogging.

Feedback and Reflection

In this chapter, teachers are guided in implementing a variety of strategies for checking student understanding, giving feedback, and stimulating reflection.

Games

Using games as a learning strategy can easily engage students. This chapter presents an array successful games that can be employed in the classroom for a variety of learning objectives.

Instructional Technology — Any Time

Any Time technologies are those applications that can be used beyond the time limits of the classroom. This chapter delineates on-line etiquette and uses of any-time technology. It describes specific technologies including blogging, virtual communities, microblogs, and wikis.

Instructional Technology — Real Time

Real Time technology refers to technologies that are used during the regular class period. The chapter gives examples with their uses.

Learning Centers

This chapter describes a variety of uses for learning centers, such as those for literacy, inquiry and exploration, differentiated instruction, sequential student-centered learning, and so on.

Logical and Independent Thinking

This chapter defines critical, creative, and persuasive thinking and presents activities to develop them. These strategies are specifically designed to raise the level of student thinking.

Manipulatives and Models

Both real and virtual manipulatives are addressed. The chapter explains why they are useful and describes general strategies for incorporating them into instruction.

Physical Movement

Physical movement can be used to address all standards, all content areas, improve test scores, and profoundly affect life skills. This chapter describes strategies for incorporating physical movement into the classroom.

Play

This chapter explains the benefits of play in promoting learning and defines categories of play that can be useful learning strategies.

Service Learning

Service learning enables students to connect academic learning to practical, everyday problems. This chapter offers suggestions for planning service learning and lists specific project ideas. It emphasizes the need for reflection throughout the process to help students see the connections between their service learning and their classroom learning.

Storytelling

This chapter describes how to use storytelling as a learning strategy. It defines storytelling skills, provides storytelling ideas, and gives teacher tips.

Summarizing

This chapter explains the benefits of summaries, suggests methods to teach summarizing, and describes some specific types of summarizing, such as best test, one-word summaries, and think-pair-share summaries.

Teaching Others

Teaching others can be an effective strategy for enabling students to learn by teaching others. The chapter identifies some opportunities for teaching others, and gives examples of peer teaching activities.

Test Preparation

This chapter discusses how to create a testing environment and how to reduce student test-anxiety, and it provides tips for helping students respond to different types of test questions.

Video

Video can be a useful strategy for introducing new materials. This chapter suggests ways to enable student learning before, during, and after instructions. It also discusses ways to access videos and the legal aspects of using them. It provides a list of video sources.

Writing to Learn

Writing to learn activities are informal writing assignments that promote student assessment of content they are involved with. Strategies described include double-entry journals, thinking cubes, inside/outside circles, narratives, RAFT, and jigsaws.

 # Introduction

To the Teacher

Teaching is a craft practiced by skilled professionals, not an exact science in which any person can follow a standard recipe that guarantees success. Even the best teaching recommendations don't work in every situation for every student. Successful teachers not only teach well, but are also able to make good decisions about what strategies work in various situations. Successful teachers also learn through experience what works in various instructional activities.

Instead of relying solely on trial and error, this teacher handbook provides a resource for continuous improvement of your craft. The summary of instructional strategies helps you add to your professional "toolkit."

This resource also helps you analyze the variables in teaching situations and systematically select strategies that are likely to lead students to success. When you are comfortable and confident with several instructional strategies, you have choices in creating effective learning experiences. This gives you a much greater chance of presenting a lesson that reaches your students.

As you continue on your journey as a teacher, the suggestions in this handbook (as well as Volume 1) will help you to strengthen your professional repertoire and make good decisions about how to present material. Better decisions will lead to more motivated and engaged students. Those satisfying moments when everything works well in teaching are why most teachers joined the profession. Use the ideas in this handbook to increase your effectiveness with students.

Several important concepts are presented in this introduction that apply to all instructional strategies. The first is the Rigor/Relevance Framework®, a tool developed by the International Center for Leadership in

Education to measure the rigor and relevance of curriculum, instruction, and assessment. When you become familiar with the Framework, you will be able to use it to facilitate learning experiences for your students that are high in cognitive skill development and contain real-world applications.

Next comes the International Center's Performance Planning Model. The interrelationship of curriculum, instruction, and assessment will become more apparent to you as you explore the complex process of curriculum planning. As a part of this process, instructional strategies can motivate the learner to engage in more rigorous and relevant learning.

Using the Rigor/Relevance Framework®

The Rigor/Relevance Framework® is a tool developed by the International Center to examine curriculum, instruction, and assessment. It uses a familiar knowledge taxonomy, while encouraging a move to application of knowledge. The Rigor/Relevance Framework helps make explicit the relevance of learning to the real world, broadening the historically narrow focus on acquisition of knowledge.

The Rigor/Relevance Framework is based on two dimensions of higher standards and student achievement. One is a continuum of knowledge based on the six levels of Bloom's Taxonomy, which describes the increasingly complex ways in which we think. The low end is acquiring knowledge and being able to recall or locate that knowledge in a simple manner (acquisition level). Just as a computer conducts a word search in a word processing program, a competent person at this level can scan through thousands of bits of information in the brain to locate that desired knowledge.

Rigor/Relevance Framework®

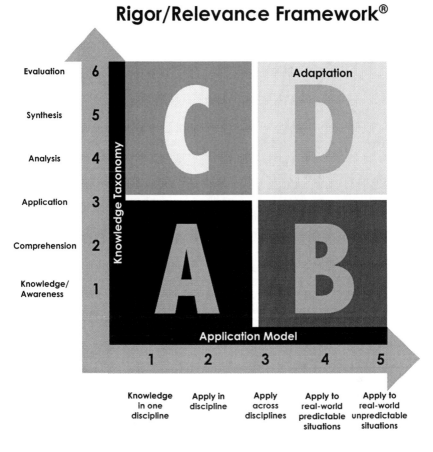

The high end of the knowledge continuum labels more complex ways in which we use knowledge. At this level, knowledge is fully integrated into our minds, and we can do much more than locate knowledge. We can take several pieces of knowledge and combine them in both logical and creative ways. Assimilation of knowledge is a good way to describe this high level of the thinking continuum. Assimilation is often referred to as a higher-order thinking skill. At this level, the student can find effective solutions to complex problems and create unique work.

The other continuum is one of action. While the knowledge continuum can be passive, the action continuum, based on the five levels of the Application Model, describes putting knowledge to use. At the low end (acquisition level), there is knowledge acquired for its own sake. At the high end of the continuum is using that knowledge to solve unpredictable problems, particularly from the real world, and to create projects, designs, and other works.

Together, the Knowledge Taxonomy and Application Model form the Rigor/Relevance Framework. A more extensive discussion of the Rigor/Relevance Framework can be found in *Using Rigor and Relevance to Create Effective Instruction*, published by the International Center. This handbook also includes activities for understanding how to use the Framework in planning curriculum and assessment.

The Rigor/Relevance Framework has four quadrants. Quadrant A represents simple recall and basic understanding of knowledge for its own sake. Directly above is Quadrant C, which represents more complex thinking, but still knowledge for its own sake. Examples of Quadrant A knowledge are knowing that the world is round and that Shakespeare wrote *Hamlet*. Quadrant C embraces higher levels of knowledge, such as knowing how the U.S. political system works and analyzing the benefits and challenges of the cultural diversity of this nation versus other nations.

Quadrants B and D represent action or high degrees of application. Quadrant B would include knowing how to use math skills to make purchases and count change. The ability to access information in wide-area network systems and gather knowledge from a variety of sources to solve a complex problem in the workplace is an example of Quadrant D knowledge.

These examples are skills in technical reading and writing.

Quadrant A: Define vocabulary terms needed to understand content of a classroom simulation.

Quadrant B: Complete a simulation following the directions given by the instructor.

Quadrant C: Compare and contrast the information gained from two simulations with that gained from reading a text on the same topic.

Quadrant D: Synthesize information from a range of sources (e.g., texts, media sources, simulations), presenting solutions to conflicting information.

Each of these four quadrants can be labeled with a term that characterizes the learning or student performance that occurs there.

Quadrant A — Acquisition

Students gather and store bits of knowledge and information. Students are primarily expected to remember or understand this acquired knowledge.

Quadrant B — Application

Students use acquired knowledge to solve problems, design solutions, and complete work. The highest level of application is to apply appropriate knowledge to new and unpredictable situations.

Quadrant C — Assimilation

Students extend and refine their knowledge so that they can use it automatically and routinely to analyze and solve problems and create solutions.

Quadrant D — Adaptation

Students have the competence to think in complex ways and also to apply knowledge and skills they have acquired. Even when confronted with perplexing unknowns, students are able to use their extensive knowledge base and skills to create unique solutions and take action that further develops their skills and knowledge.

In 2001 Bloom's Knowledge Taxonomy was updated and revised by Lorin Anderson, a student of Bloom's, and David Krathwohl, a colleague, to reflect the movement to standards-based curricula and assessment. Nouns in Bloom's original model were changed to verb forms (for example, *knowledge* to *remembering* and *comprehension* to *understanding*) and slightly reordered. We believe that the original Bloom's taxonomy as shown in our Rigor/Relevance Framework clearly describes expectations for Quadrants A, B, C, and D. The revised Bloom's elevates the importance of Quadrants B and D and indicates how 21st-century lessons should be built. We regard both the original and revised taxonomies as necessary and important.

The Rigor/Relevance Framework is easy to understand. With its simple, straightforward structure, it can serve as a bridge between school and the community. It offers a common language with which to express the notion of more rigorous and relevant standards and encompasses much of what parents, business leaders, and community members want students to learn.

The Framework is versatile; you can use it in the development of instruction and assessment. Likewise, you can use it to measure your progress in adding rigor and relevance to instruction and to select appropriate instructional strategies to meet learner needs and higher achievement goals.

Planning Instruction

To attain higher levels of rigor and relevance, instruction and assessment must not be separate and linear, but rather interrelated. Good learning takes place when there is a dynamic linkage of all components. In rigorous and relevant learning, instruction and assessment should have significant overlap. Authentic assessment should occur naturally as part of the instructional process. The current assessment reform movement seeks to place greater emphasis on student performance as opposed to simply recall of facts. Planning good instruction and assessment is easier if you abandon the image of linear progression of assessment following instruction.

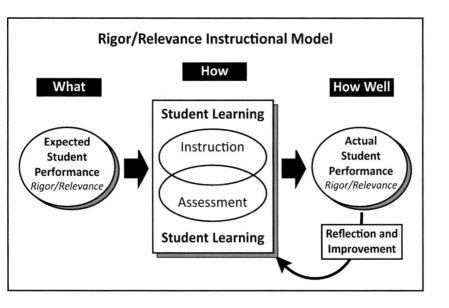

Curriculum planning occurs prior to instruction and assessment. Without effective planning, there is little likelihood that students will achieve the expected rigorous and relevant learning. Curriculum planning is a complex process. It is much more than picking out a work of literature or a textbook chapter and deciding that it would make a good instructional topic. Teacher experience and student data should be considered in order to make thoughtful decisions about instruction and assessment.

When teachers hear the word "curriculum," they generally think of unit or lesson plans that describe teaching procedures and/or student activities that would take place in a classroom. It is natural to think about these plans and immediately jump to imagine what they would look like in their classrooms. Teachers are under constant pressure to present activities that engage students, and there is little time to do much planning — such is the structure of the U.S. education system.

While curriculum must be organized into unit plans and lessons plans, curriculum planning does not begin with them. Teachers who begin and end their curriculum planning by writing a lesson plan miss important curriculum decisions.

The curriculum is a means to an end: a performance by the student. Teachers typically focus on a particular topic (e.g., volume of three-dimensional figures), use a particular resource (e.g., Periodic Table of Elements), and choose specific instructional methods (e.g., problem-based learning) to cause learning that meets a given standard. However, each of these decisions is actually a step in a learning process that should end in a performance by the student to demonstrate learning. Student activity without an end performance in mind is often busy work. Instruction, no matter how engaging or intellectual, is only beneficial if it ends with students demonstrating their knowledge and skills resulting from the learning experience. A performance approach to curriculum planning should begin with the specific student performance.

This backwards approach to curricular design also departs from another unfortunate but common practice: thinking about assessment as something to plan at the end, after teaching is completed. Rather than creating assessments near the conclusion of a unit of study (or relying on the tests provided by textbook publishers, which may not assess state standards completely or appropriately), backwards design calls for thinking about the work students will produce and how it might be assessed as you begin to plan a unit or course. Once you focus on a clear student performance, it is easier to select appropriate instructional strategies that will help students achieve that performance.

There are four major steps in planning rigorous and relevant instruction:

1. Define the focus of learning.
2. Create the student performance.
3. Design the assessment.
4. Develop the learning experiences.

The four steps are presented in the order in which ideal planning should occur. You select appropriate strategies in Step 4, after defining the focus, student performance, and assessment.

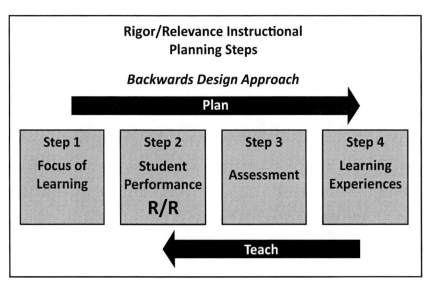

Selecting Strategies

The appropriateness of using any of the instructional strategies described in this handbook in individual situations depends upon matching the characteristics of the strategy, the learners, and what needs to be learned. All of these factors should be considered when selecting the best strategy for the learning situation. The more familiar you are with the strategies, the more likely you are to select the best strategy.

Although each strategy is described separately, the strategies are rarely used independently. When creating instructional units, you will typically select several strategies. For example, a lecture may precede a demonstration and ultimately lead to a problem-based exercise. Keeping in mind the strengths of each strategy will help you to create effective instructional experiences for your students.

Instructional Strategies and the Rigor/Relevance Framework

The first criterion to consider in selecting strategies is the level of student performance. When students are expected to demonstrate high levels of complex use of knowledge, then the instructional strategy used must give students experience with complex use of knowledge. In contrast, if students are only expected to recall knowledge, then the selected strategy can be simple, straightforward instruction. High levels of student performance often require application of knowledge.

Again, the instruction needs to match this level of expectation and give students learning experiences in which they apply knowledge.

The best way to develop a systematic approach to matching instructional strategy to the expected level of student performance is through the knowledge taxonomy and application model in the Rigor/Relevance Framework. The instructional strategies can be related to a particular quadrant of the Rigor/Relevance Framework. Likewise, the expected levels of student performance can be related to the Rigor/Relevance Framework. Select instructional strategies that work best for the quadrant in which your student objectives are located. When used at the right time, these strategies can help students to achieve expected standards. In the following chart, each strategy is rated as to its appropriateness for each of the four quadrants.

A version of this graphic appears on the first page of the description of each strategy. The more stars in a quadrant of the Rigor/Relevance Framework, the more ideal the strategy is for teaching at that level.

Instructional Strategies and the Rigor/Relevance Framework®

Strategy	Acquisition Quadrant A	Assimilation Quadrant C	Application Quadrant B	Adaptation Quadrant D
Artistic Expression	★★	★★	★★★	★★★
Compare and Contrast	★★	★	★★★	★★
Digital Media Production	★★	★★★	★★	★★★
Feedback and Reflection	★★★	★★★	★★★	★★★
Games	★★★	★★	★	★
Instructional Technology — Any Time	★★	★★	★★★	★★★
Instructional Technology — Real Time	★★★	★★★	★★	★★
Learning Centers	★★★	★★★	★★	★★
Logical and Independent Thinking	★★	★★	★★★	★★★
Manipulatives and Models	★★★	★★★	★★★	★★
Physical Movement	★★	★★★	★★	★★
Play	★	★★	★★	★★★
Service Learning	★	★★★	★★	★★★
Storytelling	★★	★★★	★★★	★★★
Summarizing	★★	★★	★★★	★★
Teaching others	★★	★★★	★★	★★★
Test Preparation	★★★	★★	★	★
Video	★★	★★★	★★	★★
Writing to Learn	★★	★★	★★★	★★★

Key   ★★★ Ideal Strategy   ★★ Appropriate Strategy
★ Least Appropriate Strategy

Note: The graphic on the first page of each strategy corresponds to this chart.

Instructional Strategies and Learning Styles

One factor to consider in selecting instructional strategies is students' learning styles. Certain strategies are more effective with a particular learning style. When matched to students' learning styles, these strategies can help students achieve at higher levels. Four broad categories of learning styles are listed below.

Concrete-Sequential learners respond to well-organized instruction that requires them to recall and construct correct responses.

Abstract-Sequential learners respond to more collaborative instruction that requires them to analyze information and explain answers.

Concrete-Random learners respond to opportunities to be creative and design products and individual responses.

Abstract-Random learners respond to creative learning activities.

In the following chart, each strategy is rated as to its usefulness for each of the four learning styles.

Instructional Strategies and Learning Styles

Strategy	Concrete-Sequential	Abstract-Sequential	Concrete-Random	Abstract-Random
Artistic Expression	★★	★★	★★★	★★★
Compare and Contrast	★★	★★★	★★	★
Digital Media Production	★	★★	★★★	★★★
Feedback and Reflection	★★	★★★	★★	★★
Games	★★★	★★	★★★	★★

Instructional Strategies and Learning Styles

Strategy	Concrete-Sequential	Abstract-Sequential	Concrete-Random	Abstract-Random
Instructional Technology – Any Time	★★★	★★★	★★★	★★★
Instructional Technology – Real Time	★★★	★★	★★★	★★
Learning Centers	★★	★★	★★★	★★★
Logical and Independent Thinking	★★★	★★★	★★★	★★
Manipulatives and Models	★★	★★	★★★	★★
Physical Movement	★★	★★★	★★	★★★
Play	★★	★★★	★★★	★★★
Service Learning	★★	★★★	★★	★★★
Storytelling	★★	★★★	★★★	★★★
Summarizing	★★★	★★★	★★	★
Teaching Others	★★★	★★★	★★	★★
Test Preparation	★★★	★★	★	★
Video	★★★	★★★	★★★	★★
Writing to Learn	★★★	★★★	★★	★★★

Key   ★★★ Ideal Strategy   ★★ Appropriate Strategy
★ Least Appropriate Strategy

Instructional Strategies and Assessment

Various types of assessments can be used to measure what a student knows and is able to do. Learning through a particular instructional strategy is best measured by an assessment type that parallels the strategy. Making a conscious effort to mirror instruction in assessment will enhance the student's ability to perform.

The following chart correlates the appropriateness of the instructional strategies to the eight most frequently used types of assessment.

Types of Assessment

- Multiple Choice
- Constructed Response
- Extended Response
- Process Performance
- Product Performance
- Portfolio
- Interview
- Self-reflection

Instructional Strategies and Assessment

Strategy	Multiple Choice	Constructed Response	Extended Response	Process Performance	Product Performance	Portfolio	Interview	Self-reflection
Artistic Expression	★	★	★★	★★	★★★	★★★	★★	★★
Compare and Contrast	★★	★★★	★★★	★★	★★	★	★	★
Digital Media Production	★★	★★	★★	★★★	★★★	★★★	★★★	★★
Feedback and Reflection	★★	★★★	★★★	★★★	★★	★★	★★★	★★
Games	★★★	★★★	★	★★	★	★	★	★★
Instructional Technology—Any Time	★★	★★	★★	★★★	★★★	★★★	★★	★★
Instructional Technology—Real Time	★★	★★★	★★	★★★	★★★	★★	★	★★
Learning Centers	★★★	★★★	★★★	★★	★★	★★★	★★	★★★
Logical and Independent Thinking	★	★★	★★★	★★★	★★	★★★	★★★	★★★
Manipulatives and Models	★	★	★★	★★★	★★★	★★	★★	★★
Physical Movement	★	★	★★	★★★	★★	★	★★★	★★★
Play	★	★	★★	★★★	★★	★★	★★★	★★★
Service Learning	★	★	★★	★★	★★	★★★	★★★	★★★
Storytelling	★	★	★★★	★★★	★★★	★★★	★★★	★★
Summarizing	★	★★	★★★	★★	★★★	★★★	★★	★★

Instructional Strategies and Assessment (Continued)

Teaching Others	★★	★★	★★	★★★	★★	★★	★★★	★★★
Test Preparation	★★★	★★★	★★	★★	★★	★★	★★	★★
Video	★★★	★★★	★★	★★	★★	★★	★★	★★
Writing to Learn	★	★★	★★★	★★★	★★★	★★★	★★★	★★★

Key ★★★ Ideal Strategy   ★★ Appropriate Strategy
★ Least Appropriate Strategy

Instructional Strategies and Educational Technology

A continuing debate centers on whether technology is the panacea that will help many students learn at higher levels or an exciting fad that is a temporary distraction from the real process of learning. The potential is there for either outcome. The degree to which technology has positive impacts on learning depends on the way it is applied in the classroom and beyond.

When used effectively, technology offers exciting possibilities for expanding learning beyond what schools have taught before. Technology accommodates various learning styles. Technology puts vast amounts of knowledge at students' fingertips. Information on every subject imaginable is available for study in all curriculum areas.

Technology offers students a chance to delve deeply into subjects. Greater accessibility to information gives students the opportunity to gather data easily and analyze and synthesize it in new ways. Students can manipulate data to identify those portions that are relevant to their needs. They can integrate data from one subject area to another and use the information to enhance their understanding.

Technology links curriculum with real-world experiences both inside and outside school. Using telecommunications and computer networks, students can work together in cooperative learning situations to help solve real problems, tying their education to real-life situations and giving them invaluable learning experiences.

Technology gives you a tool to create your own teaching materials, to go beyond required textbooks and use alternate resources, and to reorganize information in new ways. Students can also manipulate and reorder what they learn, giving them greater control over their learning.

Technology can enhance any of the instructional strategies. The following chart lists a few ways that education technology can be used with each of the strategies.

Instructional Strategies and Educational Technology*

Strategy	Application of Technology
Artistic Expression	• Compose songs using electronic instruments. • Record and play music with technology. • Create displays using drawing and painting software. • Record and edit digital photos and video.
Compare and Contrast	• Use graphic organizers on computers to record and display relationships.
Feedback and Reflection	• Communicate with students outside of class using technology. • Students keep electronic journals.
Games	• Use digital response pads or smart phones for response. • Use projectors or interactive white boards for display. • Use electronic versions of games.
Learning Centers	• Create learning center activities using a technology application.
Logical and Independent Thinking	• Student support logical arguments using digital slides and video.

Instructional Strategies and Educational Technology*

Strategy	Application of Technology
Manipulatives and Models	• Student create digital model. • Use digital models for demonstrations.
Physical Movement	• Record movements with video.
Play	• Use technology as unstructured activity for students to explore and experiment.
Service Learning	• Use social networks for students to record their experiences, reflect on learning and discussing with other students. • Use Internet to locate and connect students and service project sites.
Storytelling	• Students use computer-based tools in storytelling.
Summarizing	• Organize notes and references using software. • Create digital graphic organizers to summarize information. • Use word processing to rewrite summaries. • Use wikis to create summaries with other students.
Teaching Others	• Tutor other students using online conferencing software.
Test Preparation	• Set up computer-based flash cards to practice recall. • Use computer based practice test questions.
Writing to Learn	• Write and submit a project via computer.

*The strategies Digital Media Production, Instructional Technology — Any Time, Instructional Technology — Real Time, and Video are not included in this chart because they always involve technology.

KNOWLEDGE

APPLICATION

Artistic Expression

The Arts as Subject and Strategy

The arts are frequently identified as a separate subject area, generally including four sub-categories: music, dance, drama and visual arts. Each of these areas has national and state standards that have helped to affirm the arts as important subject areas. However, the arts are generally considered elective subjects often competing for time within the tight schedule of a school day.

Fewer than half the states require a half unit of course credit or more in the arts for high school graduation. Whether or not art courses are a requirement at the state level, they are typically offered as electives at the high school level. However, as both graduation and college entrance requirements increase, even students who wish to pursue a career in the art field are finding it more difficult to take an elective class in the arts.

Even in elementary schools educators struggle with how much time to devote to core academic instruction, perceived to lead directly to performance on high-stakes exams, versus how much time to allocate to the arts. However, this does not have to be an either/or choice; look for opportunities for students to be engaged in the arts while working toward academic achievement.

School leaders and policymakers are unlikely to make dramatic shifts in the core academic requirements and testing programs: language arts, mathematics, and science will be priorities for a long time. However, not every student has to achieve those core skills in the same manner. When teachers use arts as a strategy, they often increase student engagement and increase academic achievement.

The Arts Help Improve Academics

In 1995 the United States Department of Education reported in, *Schools, Communities, and the Arts: A Research Compendium*, that "using arts processes to teach academic subjects results not only in improved understanding of content but it greatly improved self-regulatory behavior." Often, students who struggle in schools with direct instruction based primarily on verbal skills are more comfortable in a classroom that emphasizes artistic processes and activities. This might involve movement in dance or theater or the opportunity to produce images in the visual arts.

Brain research reinforces the premise of seeking greater integration of the arts and academics. The human brain is incredibly complex, yet the way that educators in many academic areas approach instruction assumes that the brain is a simple device for storage and retrieval of information. We give students information through lecture and reading and expect students to recall that information and fill in short-answer questions. However, the neural connections that make remembering and solving problems possible require a rich, stimulating environment, strong emotional connections, and individual choice. The typical artistic activity, rich in movement, song, or color, is naturally stimulating to the human brain.

We have known for a long time that there are significant differences in how students learn. Some students learn effectively by listening and do very well in traditional classrooms where most of the information is presented orally. However, this is less than a quarter of the students in any classroom. The majority of students are visual learners who use illustrations, charts, diagrams, and words to build understanding. Many students are kinesthetic learners who may have difficulty understanding concepts until they are able to work with manipulatives or experience concrete examples. The arts offer valuable experiences to facilitate student learning for both visual and kinesthetic learners.

Dr. Howard Gardner developed the theory of multiple intelligences, suggesting that our school systems primarily teach, test, and reinforce only two kinds of intelligence — verbal and logical/mathematical. Gardner further proposed that at least five other kinds of intelligence are equally as important: visual/spatial, kinesthetic, musical, interpersonal, and intrapersonal. These additional intelligences are the foundations for the various areas of the arts. When students have an opportunity to participate in the areas of the arts, these personal strengths and intelligences emerge.

Visual Arts

Students today are growing up in a highly visual world surrounded by images on television as well as in videos, advertising displays, and other media. The area of the human brain that records visual information is five times larger than the area that records auditory information, so the positive response of students to visual stimulation is both natural and powerful. In addition, current technological tools make it easy for a wider variety of students to create and share visual information. High school students can use the visual arts to design sets for various scenes of a Shakespearean play. Middle school students can read about the culture of another country and create and share three-dimensional objects that represent that culture. In elementary schools students can illustrate colorful timelines with pictures of historical events that they discover throughout the year. At all levels, students can produce multimedia reports that include drawings, paintings, photographs, and other illustrations. Student work does need not to be limited to written words. Consider ways students can create visual works to demonstrate learning. More information on digital media student work is available in the Digital Media chapter in this handbook.

Music

Humans are rhythmical by nature. We have our own natural rhythms of breathing and pulse. We are surrounded by music every day and enjoy it for relaxation or motivation. Music not only engages our personal rhythms, it touches our human emotions. The ability to recognize patterns in mathematics is the same intellectual skill that allows students to recognize and perform patterns in music. In fact, many of the world's leading researchers in engineering and complex mathematics are also musicians.

Children learn basic skills such as the alphabet through music. Like many of the other arts, learning to play an instrument or compose music requires concentration, practice, and discipline before achieving a performance or a product. Making music together in an orchestra or choir helps to develop collaborative skills that are useful throughout life. The skills learned through music can be applied to many areas of learning.

Dance

Brain circuitry research helps us better understand the connection between movement and intellectual development. Having students sit quietly at a desk actually causes their brain to shut down rather than be stimulated. In dance, practicing and learning complex rhythmical patterns stimulates and energizes the whole mind-body system. Kinesthetic students, who need to move to learn, often find opportunities to do so in acceptable ways through dance. Dance creates strong, coordinated, and well-disciplined bodies that can move with grace and individual style. A student preparing to give a dance performance must memorize the choreography, rehearse, and collaborate with other dancers. By doing this, students develop critical thinking skills along with persistence and perseverance. Students can use simple dance and movement as a way to engage and remember new concepts.

Drama

Drama is a natural extension of literature. It includes taking written text and transforming language into vivid scenes and individual performance. Formal theater helps to develop additional skills in areas of creating sets, costumes, props, lighting design, and scripts. Memorization of lines helps reinforce academic achievement. Drama becomes a much more engaging way for students to bring literature to life and to develop self-confidence in expression and working with others.

Examples of Lessons to Integrate Academics

The following are examples of lessons that integrate academics with areas of the arts. Use these lesson plans to stimulate your thinking of the possibilities of using art to teach academic areas. (ArtsEdge Lesson Plans)

English Language Arts

Character Life Box

Students work in pairs to create a "life box" of a character in a play. They collect five props, a costume piece, or clues about the character and write a poem about the character. Other students must interpret the clues and determine which character is represented by the life box.

A Way with Words

Shakespeare invented over 2,000 words and expressive phrases. Students use drawing and pantomime to identify and analyze some of Shakespeare's phrases. They then write a story using the newly identified words, lines, and phrases.

Characterization in Literature

In this lesson, students explore various methods authors use to create effective characters. Students consider what makes a character believable and create their own characterizations. They also write a short script using the characters they created and act out the script.

Mathematics

Creating "AB" Patterns

Patterns exist both in the natural and human-made world. They are an element in art as well as math. Knowledge of patterns allows the learner to systematize and predict outcomes. In an activity to examine patterns in fabrics, students construct this concept using visual arts designs and math manipulatives.

Hats Off To Color

Early elementary students learn about primary and secondary colors. They experiment with mixing primary colors in proportions and then demonstrate their understanding using simple equations and creative movement and dramatization.

First Rhythmic Composition

Students are introduced to rhythm concepts, including the names and symbols associated with music notation. Students fill in a chart that outlines names and meanings of rhythmic musical symbols. Using these symbols, they clap rhythm sequences and compose their first compositions. They also compare these rhythmic sequences to math concepts.

Science

Animal Habitats

Early primary students learn about animal habitats. Students use chronological ordering and phonics to reinforce beginning literacy skills. They demonstrate understanding of these concepts through song, movement, and creative dramatization.

What Is Inside a Cell?

In this lesson, students gain an understanding of the components of a cell. They match definitions of organelles with the organelle name, research the organelle's form and function, and contribute to a class drawing of a cell by depicting a specific organelle within the composite cell. Through this lesson, students explore answers to the essential question: How are "form" and "function" related in biology?

Oxidation and Combustion: Chemical Reactions in Fire

Students explore concepts such as exothermic and endothermic reactions, combustion, and oxidation-reduction reactions through fireworks. Students make predictions about the results of oxidation-reduction reactions that occur with a candle's flame. They also conduct online activities to learn how firework shells are made. Finally, students learn about the art of creating fireworks displays. They learn design concepts such as repetition, emphasis, and balance. Students can use online tools to design their own firework displays.

Atomic and Molecular Structure

Students use knowledge of basic physical science concepts to create movement patterns that simulate the movement of atoms and molecules. They formulate and answer questions about how movement choices communicate abstract ideas in dance and demonstrate an understanding of how personal experience influences the interpretation of a dance.

Multiple Disciplines

Can You Measure Up?

After reading the book *Cook-A-Doodle-Doo!*, primary students engage in dramatization and a variety of measuring activities that include estimation, equivalents, and elapsed time. Students work collaboratively to conduct measuring "experiments", record their findings, and present their findings in final reports.

How Many Cells Are Born in a Day?

In this lesson, students use calculators or pencils to predict the number of cells that result from a series of cell divisions. They then graph the results to represent their findings. Students use this investigation as a starting point for an exploration of pattern and repetition in nature, culminating with an activity in which they create a repeated or random pattern of their own. This lesson helps students gain an understanding of how patterns are reflected in nature.

Oceans: A Fact Haiku

The sound and movement of ocean waves may be called poetry in motion. Oceans can be used to teach students about a form of Japanese poetry. After learning about a haiku and hearing a haiku, students listen to the ocean to inspire them in writing their own haiku.

Songs from the Past

Songs about events, times, and places in history have been passed down from generation to generation. Students explore historical songs and analyze lyrics in order to learn about historical times and happenings. Students are introduced to composers and their music as they explore these historical events. Finally, students survey family, friends, and neighbors to determine what they know about historical songs and represent the findings in the form of graphs and charts.

Art Apprenticeship in the Renaissance

Students follow the apprenticeship model to learn to make paints from egg yolk and paint three-dimensional objects in a two-dimensional painting using geometrical mathematics and linear perspective.

Creating Postage Stamps

Students create an original and authentic piece of art in the style of a U.S. postal stamp to represent their selected state. After completing research and brainstorming activities, the student draws thumbnail sketches to determine the best design layout using art skills relating to the elements and principles of design.

Resources

Learning Through the Arts — www.ltta.ca Website with lesson plans and resources from the Royal Conservatory of Music — Canada

Artally — www.artally.org Arts advocacy site.

Arts Education Partnership — www.aep-arts.org Provides information and communication about current and emerging arts education policies, issues, and activities at the national, state, and local levels.

References

ArtsEdge Lesson Plans. http://artsedge.kennedy-center.org/educators/lessons.aspx Retrieved April 2012

Gardner, H. *Frames of Mind.* New York: Basic Books, 1987

Schools, Communities, and the Arts: A Research Compendium. http://morrisoninstitute.asu.edu/publications-reports/SchoolsCommunitiesAndArts-AResearchCompendium/view Retrieved August 2010

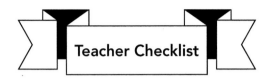

Teacher Checklist

Yes	No	
☐	☐	Teachers from the arts and academic areas have opportunities to plan together.
☐	☐	Art teachers are familiar with academic standards.
☐	☐	Team teaching occurs occasionally between art and academic teachers.
☐	☐	Academic teachers observe classes in the arts to discover interdisciplinary applications.
☐	☐	Activities in the arts are designed for students to apply academic skills.
☐	☐	Art activities are aligned with appropriate academic standards.
☐	☐	Students who are naturally kinesthetic or visual learners are identified in the classroom.
☐	☐	A variety of activities are designed that appeal to kinesthetic and visual learners.
☐	☐	Students are given the opportunity to create visual products to express points of view.
☐	☐	Students are given the opportunity to express themselves musically or in dance.
☐	☐	Students are given the opportunity to express themselves in dramatic productions.

APPLICATION

Compare and Contrast

What Is Compare and Contrast?

Compare and contrast is analysis to identify similarities and differences among objects, ideas, people, and events. A process used to classify, sort, and discover patterns, compare and contrast is frequently implemented when analyzing text and encourages students to discover knowledge for themselves during individual or small group work. In addition, the process of analyzing sets of data, such as numbers in a math class or statistical information in social studies, is useful in teaching how to evaluate and synthesize information.

The overarching purpose of using compare and contrast is to raise the level of rigor of thinking. In 2001 Bloom's Knowledge Taxonomy was updated and revised by Lorin Anderson, one of Bloom's students, and colleague David Krathwohl to reflect the movement to standards-based curricula and assessment. Nouns in Bloom's original model were changed to verb forms (for example, *knowledge* to *remembering* and *com-*

prehension to *understanding*) and slightly reordered. The original taxonomy shown in the Rigor/Relevance Framework describes expectations for Quadrants A, B, C, and D. The revised taxonomy elevates the importance of Quadrants B and D and indicates how 21st-century lessons should be built. Both the original and revised taxonomies are necessary and important.

Quadrant D on the Rigor/Relevance Framework is the quadrant in which students have the competence to think in complex ways and also apply knowledge and skills they have acquired. When you guide student thinking to Quadrant D, you place more emphasis on student learning and application. Compare and contrast is one of the strategies correlated with achievement because of the rigorous thinking involved (Marzano).

Compare and contrast is used to help students identify language cues, clarify thinking, and define ideas. When students see words in text such as *on the other hand, but, however, yet,* and *nevertheless,* they should identify these words as signals to make a comparison or a contrast with the information presented. Students can also learn how to compare and contrast without reading large passages of text using the strategies presented in this chapter. You can use compare and contrast in all grade levels and in all subject areas.

Using Compare and Contrast: Graphic Organizers

One way to use compare and contrast in your classroom is to have students create a graphic organizer. The student creates a graphic organizer after direct instruction, such as listening, reading, or viewing information. After the students complete the graphic organizers, a discussion is helpful so that you can help students synthesize and evaluate the information.

Alike and Different

Select two pairs of words and have a brainstorming session with the whole group. You can ask students to give answers in short phrases or in complete sentences. Remind students (especially in Grades K–3) that when we *compare,* we show how things are alike and when we *contrast,* we show how they are different.

Model #1: Chair — Dog

Alike	Different
four legs	something you sit on — animal
nouns	silent — makes noise

Model #2: Martin Luther King, Jr. — Abraham Lincoln

Alike	Different
both men who fought for civil rights	not a U.S. president — U.S. president
	lived in 20th century — lived in 19th century

1. After you model the process, arrange the students in pairs or small groups. Ask students to divide a sheet of paper down the middle and label the left column *Alike* and the right column *Different.*

2. Provide students with several pairs of words and allow them to use resources in the classroom to help them find facts. Share a graphic organizer that has been completed for one pair of words.

3. Remind students to cite the source(s) they use to write facts.

Cause and Effect

You can also use a two-column table for a cause-and-effect activity. This strategy helps students identify more with contrast than compare, so it solidifies the importance of identifying how and why things are different. Model two examples of both cause and effect for the students. After they have seen two examples, leave one side of the table blank and brainstorm ideas.

Cause	Effect
I set my alarm clock for PM instead of AM.	I was late for school today.
I stuck a pin into a balloon.	The balloon popped.
Snow fell one foot an hour during a big storm.	???
???	I scored a 100% on the math test.

1. After you model the process, arrange the students in pairs or small groups. Ask students to divide a sheet of paper down the middle and label the left column *Cause* and the right column *Effect*.

2. Provide students with several sentences that are written on index cards and placed in two separate piles (one for cause and one for effect). Ask pairs or groups of students to draw two cards from each pile without looking.

3. Tell the students to write their sentences in the appropriate column, then discuss possible causes and effects for the given situation.

Venn Diagram

The most common use of a Venn diagram is in math. It shows the relationship between and among sets. You can use two circles or three circles, depending upon the concept you are teaching and how much information needs to be organized. You can also use it in other content areas to provide students with a tool for organizing information. For example, in an English class, it can be used to analyze similarities and differences in characters, stories, or poems. A Venn diagram is also an effective pre-writing activity. It helps students visually organize thoughts, quotations, similarities and differences prior to writing a compare and contrast essay.

Venn Diagram

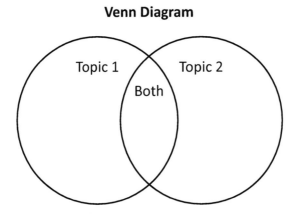

To add interest, consider showing the overlapping symbols as something other than a circle. Try to select a symbol or graphic that relates to the content of what is being analyzed. For example, elementary students might compare and contrast apples and oranges by completing a graphic organizer that shows an overlapping apple and orange. Middle school students might compare and contrast the American and French Revolution by completing a graphic that overlays the outlines of the two nations.

Compare and Contrast Between Sets

In this example from an elementary math class, students are given two sets of numbers, one of which is labeled *YES* and one of which is labeled *NO*. Their task is to determine the concept that is being taught based on the set labeled *YES*. This activity can be used as a pre-assessment strategy for you to see evidence of a student's prior knowledge, or it can be used as a post-assessment strategy to validate learning.

YES: { 2, 4, 6, 8, 10, . . .}   NO: {3, 5, 7, 9, 11, . . .}

Guiding Questions

1. What do the numbers in the first set have in common? (They are all evenly divisible by two.)
2. What do the numbers in the second set have in common? (They are not evenly divisible by two.)
3. What concept is being taught? (Even numbers)

Compare and Contrast Among Ideas, Objects, and Other Concepts

The previous section showed compare-and-contrast activities for two sets of data. In the following activities, students are given three ideas, objects, or concepts to analyze and explain similarities and differences. Instead of graphic organizers, students use their analytical skills and ability to justify their thinking.

What Does Not Belong?

Helping students analyze larger amounts of text can be facilitated through learning activities that use smaller amounts of text. In this activity, students use sets of words to identify the "oddball" word and justify why it does not belong in the set.

You will need to have a good idea about your students' prior knowledge, especially when you use this strategy in a specific content area. Be very intentional as you plan your lessons. The following example uses generic words. Ask your students to identify the word that does not belong and write an explanation about why that word does not belong. Students can use short phrases or complete sentences.

Data Set	Oddball	Explanation
1. Blue, Bus, Yellow	Bus	not a color
2. Square, Triangle, Cube	Cube	not a two-dimensional shape
3. Stove, Skateboard, Refrigerator	Skateboard	not a kitchen appliance

What Do They Have In Common?

In this activity, all three words belong in the same category. You can structure this learning activity in the following two ways:

1. Provide the students with the names of each of the categories but not in the correct order.

2. Do not provide the students with the names of each of the categories. Ask them to explain the thinking process in determining the correct category. You might find that students come up with different categories from those you feel are correct. For example, the words in Set 3 could be categorized as "things you put on a hamburger" or "things you put in a salad."

Data Set	Effect
1. Albany, Buffalo, Rochester	cities in New York State
2. elephant, deer, dog	animals with four legs
3. onions, tomato, lettuce	things we grow in our garden

Analogies

The word *analogy* simply means "word relationships." This strategy is a higher-level thinking compare-and-contrast strategy and frequently appears on standardized tests, such as the SAT and the GRE. There are two common frameworks for an analogy. In each, D is usually left for the student to answer.

#1: A is to B as C is to D

#2: (A) : (B) :: (C) : (D)

Categories/relationships of analogies can include the following:

- Antonyms: UP is to DOWN as LEFT is to RIGHT
- Cause and Effect: INFECTION is to ILLNESS as CARELESSNESS is to ACCIDENT

- Descriptions: BLUE is to SKY as GREEN is to GRASS
- Parts of a Whole: FINGER is to HAND as LEAF is to TREE
- Synonyms: CALM is to SERENE as ANGRY is to MAD
- What It Is/Does: KNIFE is to CUTS as SHOVEL is to DIGS

The following are a few tips to consider when planning a lesson using analogies.

1. Decide whether you will give the students multiple-choice answers for each analogy or whether you will leave it open ended. If you leave the analogies open ended, students have more opportunities to engage in rigorous thinking.

2. Extend thinking by asking students to come up with the category for the analogy. You can provide categories for students to make connections or ask students to recall categories from examples already done in class.

The following are some examples of content-specific analogies you can use with your students.

- 6 is to 36 as 9 is to ____
- CONIFEROUS is to CONE as DECIDUOUS is to _____
- OBAMA is to BIDEN as BUSH is to _____
- NOUN is to PERSON as VERB is to _____
- BASEBALL is to INNINGS as FOOTBALL is to _____
- PAINTER is to WATERCOLORS as POTTER is to _____
- MOZART is to CLASSICAL as LED ZEPPELIN is to _____

Metaphors and Similes

A metaphor is an implied analogy, and a simile is an expressed one. A metaphor compares two unlike things often using forms of the verb *to be*. A simile shows a comparison using the words *like* or *as*. Students can apply the compare-and-contrast strategy when they are given examples of metaphors and similes. The following are some examples:

- Metaphor: His glare was the ice that brought me to shiver.
- Simile: She is as cold as ice.
- Metaphor: Juliet is the sun.
- Simile: Juliet's smile is as bright as the sun.
- Metaphor: Math is a walk in park!
- Simile: Solving this equation is as easy as pie.

Extending Learning Beyond Compare and Contrast

Making Predictions

Comparing and contrasting information can help students make predictions. Students can use their prior knowledge about a situation and compare it to a current situation that they are analyzing.

- Situation: You are in science class and need to determine which objects will float. You have a plastic milk jug and a brick. How can you use compare and contrast to determine which object will float?

- Situation: You observe that the sky has turned dark and big gray clouds are gathering. What season is it? Is it more likely to rain or snow?

- Situation: A new law is passed that requires teenagers to take driving courses at night. What is the difference between driving during the day and driving at night?

Sequencing

When we want to build reading and writing skills, using sequencing can help students arrange their thinking in chronological order. Students need to become familiar with certain words that signal a specific sequence: *first, next, then,* and *finally*. As students become more familiar with signal words, they can learn to compare and contrast the signal words to sort out the difference among the beginning, middle, and end. The following are some examples of how you might use sequencing.

1. Provide a list of signal words and ask students to write their own short story that has a definitive beginning, middle, and end.
2. Have students read a passage that is written out of order and ask them to rearrange it in chronological order.
3. Write events separately (perhaps on index cards) and ask students to arrange them in the order in which they occurred.

Patterns

Compare and contrast is useful in mathematics when students are first learning how to recognize patterns and in later grades when they are asked to extend and describe patterns. Patterns can include sets of numbers, shapes, or letters.

To encourage more rigorous thinking, expose students to a wider variety of number patterns whose rules are less obvious. For example, look at these patterns and find the missing terms:

Pattern #1: 24, 21, 18, 15, ____
Pattern #2: 9, 12, 15, 18, ____

Guiding Questions

1. Compare the first two numbers.
2. Compare the second and third numbers.
3. Compare the third and fourth numbers.
4. Compare the two patterns. How are they alike? Different?

References

Marzano, R., et. al. *Classroom Instruction That Works*. Alexandria, VA: ASCD, 2001

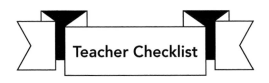

Teacher Checklist

Yes	No	
☐	☐	Grade-level appropriate strategies are employed.
☐	☐	Students are given timely feedback during independent practice.
☐	☐	Students have all the supplies necessary to successfully complete the activity.
☐	☐	The activity engages the students' prior knowledge.
☐	☐	Whole-group brainstorming allows all ideas to be accepted.
☐	☐	Students demonstrate a higher level of rigor in their thinking.
☐	☐	Students show evidence that they understand the purpose of using compare and contrast strategies.
☐	☐	Students demonstrate respectful behavior during small group work.
☐	☐	Graphic organizers are used to model strategies.
☐	☐	Students are allowed to reflect after using various graphic organizers.
☐	☐	Graphic organizers are intentionally designed prior to the lesson for easy use and application.
☐	☐	Students clearly justify their thinking.

APPLICATION

Digital Media Production

21st-Century Learning

The digital world has opened up an area of expression and assessment to educators that has endless opportunities. Students who roll their eyes at the thought of writing a five-page paper are suddenly more engaged at the thought of a video presentation or a photo story to present information.

The definition of digital media is ever expanding with new forms and new ways of sharing ideas digitally. Students help to redefine and expand the definition constantly as they use digital media in unique ways. In their daily lives, students work with digital media as they watch videos online, post to social networking sites, or rant on a blog. We need to incorporate the many ways students communicate into our curriculum.

Part of the problem teachers have with digital media is that they fear students will lose the ability to express themselves in traditional formats, such as the written word. This does not have to be the case if teachers use resources and tools wisely. Teaching students to work with digital media and use traditional skills (grammar, essay format, math skills) is crucial to creating products that truly express what students have learned. This is living in Quadrant D — High Rigor/High Relevance. Students should integrate their learned skills with their learned knowledge to embody 21st-century thinking, design, and application.

What are some possible outcomes for student digital work that can incorporate this digital energy into lessons? Instead of writing in their journal, students post to a blog. Instead of writing a 10-page paper, students make a five-minute vodcast that posts to a classroom website.

Digital media is an instantaneous and easily accessible format of self-expression that speaks to the 21st-century learner. Students of all ages are taking advantage of it. In this chapter, three primary types of digital work are reviewed: digital video, podcasting, and vodcasting, and student blogging.

Digital Video

Integrating digital video into lessons is a two-fold process: first using video in teaching and then assigning video as part of student work. The easiest way to incorporate video is by having students watch short clips that reinforce the curriculum. This can be anything from a 30-second commercial to a five-minute excerpt from a movie or news show. Using video in teaching is more extensively described in the chapter on video. Though using video may be new and exciting to you, students watch videos all of the time. Start to think outside the box regarding forms of student work.

Incorporating video into assignments starts to spark students' interests. Now the creative freedom is in the students' hands, and they get to become the producers to figure out how to convey the information in the best way possible.

Students are charged with the task of interpreting the information into a video format to demonstrate understanding and proper application of that knowledge.

Classroom Functions of Digital Video

Assessment of Learning. Digital video can assess student learning. Remember that the quality of the video may not reflect their actual knowledge. Try to look past the shaky camera work and see the content behind it.

Organization of Concepts. Students have to work with the content and organize it in a way that makes sense to others. This process helps students to deepen their understanding of the topic and teach it to others through their video.

Collaboration. Video projects are usually created by a small group of students. This type of project is a mass collaboration of ideas and talents. Students can choose a production position and offer insight from that perspective.

Writing Skills. Most video projects require a treatment (written proposal) and storyboard (descriptions with drawings). This reinforces communication skills through effective writing and graphic features. Students must effectively communicate their video ideas prior to production.

Curriculum Examples of Use of Digital Video

The following are sample digital video project ideas for different classes. Modify them to fit your curriculum, or think of variations that can be used.

Mathematics

How to Video. Have your students record voiceover and then sync it with digital pictures or video to demonstrate how to solve a math problem. The shot may only include someone's hand or pencil demonstrating the steps to solve the problem.

Word Problem Skits. Have students come up with a word problem and act it out with the steps of how to solve it using math skills.

English Language Arts

Poem Raps. Some students love to perform raps or songs. Have them select a favorite poem and set it to a beat. This usually works best in small groups and can be played back for the whole class to enjoy.

Action. The students record a short scene from a play or story. You can emphasize how the camera angle can help reveal things about a character or the scene, instead of actually having the character say the words.

History

Reenactments. Help your students understand historical figures by re-enacting a scene from history. Assign each student a role and have him or her research that historical figure. Choose a short situation in which the students have to become the historical figures. Let the action unfold in front of the camera.

Digital Slideshows. Not every project needs live video. Let students find pictures to help tell a story from history, or use pictures to do a biopic of a historical figure. These pictures can even be current if it helps to reveal things about the topic. Have the student record voiceover on top of the pictures.

Science

Talk Show Demos. Let your students pretend that they are the guest on a talk show. Have them present to the camera about one of your scientific topics. For example, they could do a demonstration about how something works or explain a current trend in the weather using tangibles or simply answering questions from the host of the show. Let students be creative and figure out the best way to present the information to a "television" audience.

Science Hunter. Let your students become the host of their own science show like the Crocodile Hunter. They can record a short segment where they talk directly to the camera about whatever it is they are discovering. For example, the show could include someone going through your lab revealing items of interest or interviews of other students to define how the lab works.

Electives

Explanations. Whether it is a dance, art piece, or piano sonata, allow students to explain their project to an audience. This helps students build a deeper understanding of their work. Student can explain their work through voiceover or a "talking head" (close-up shot of student) with video of their project playing over or between clips.

Demonstrations. In this project students demonstrate the technique or process of something related to your curriculum. This could be as simple as a three-step video on how to properly throw a baseball. Students demonstrate their understand and improve communication skills

Remember, adding video to your lessons is supposed to engage students more than traditional lessons do. If you find that it is having the opposite effect, consider revising your project guidelines.

Hints for Digital Video

- Creating a quality video takes a lot of time and some knowledge. Introduce the topic by only using digital pictures and sound. This helps students learn how to create a project before introducing recorded video.

- Spend some time in class explaining how to use a camera and a tripod properly.

- Many videos need some sort of basic editing to cut clips or add music. Fortunately, easy-to-use software applications such as iMovie (Mac) or Windows Movie Maker (PC) can create polished pieces. Use online tutorials to help you and your students start to edit.

- Students may get so excited about the project that they try to create something beyond their expertise. This creates a lot of frustration for the student and usually results in an unfinished project. Help students by setting parameters for the project like a time limit (less than 2-3 minutes). You can also limit the special features students may use (sound effects, music, titles, or special effects) to help students focus on the content of the project and not just the technology available.

- Digital storytelling is another form of expression through the use of software and video. Allow students the opportunity to tell their story using pictures, audio and video. Consider using Microsoft PowerPoint or other online resources such as Microsoft's Photo Story to help students learn to share their experiences through digital creation. By turning an everyday project into a 21st-century endeavor, students use the skills they will need in the future.

Podcasting and Vodcasting

Students of all ages are enraptured by the technology in the palm of their hand: MP3 players, iPods, and smart phones are changing society as we know it. As teachers, we are learning to tap into this technology to better reach our students. Podcasting and vodcasting are quickly finding a niche in classrooms and curriculum. Since many students now have the technology to play them, they are also more excited about learning how to create them.

A podcast is an audio file that is made available on the Internet for download and playback using a computer or a mobile device such as an iPod, MP3 Player, or smart phone. A vodcast is different from a podcast because it incorporates video as well as audio. A vodcast can be as simple as someone sitting in front of the laptop camera speaking directly to the audience. A host of available podcasts and vodcasts centered on education can be found in the iTunes University. Many students young and old are taking advantage of this technology. Consult iTunes for podcasts about how to make podcasts.

Classroom Functions for Podcasting and Vodcasting

Teaching Others. Podcasts or vodcasts provide students another way to teach others. Students can create and post short vignettes that explain how to solve a math problem or present another perspective of a historical event. Using podcasts and vodcasts to supplement teaching others is a great way to stimulate higher-level thinking and application.

Assessment. Many teachers are using podcasts and vodcasts as forms of assessment. Students demonstrate their knowledge but do it in a way that speaks to their technological generation. Assessments could include a summary assignment about a class field trip or article. Students can add models, tables, diagrams and pictures to their presentation.

Reading Fluency. Many elementary classrooms use podcasts to help strengthen reading fluency. Students record themselves reading a text and later refer back to it for self-evaluation. Teachers can also go back and check the recording later, which helps teachers who have a large class of students.

Collaborative Problem Solving. Another engaging Quadrant D activity is having students work collaboratively to create solutions to community problems or issues. Students might work with groups of students in other schools or even other nations. The podcasts and vodcasts are effective tools for students to work collaboratively.

Parent/Community Connection. Podcasts and vodcasts can help teachers share information with the community and parents. The link can be posted to your classroom webpage or school site. Showcase the work of your students.

Getting Started with Podcasting and Vodcasting

- Figure out if you have the technology needed in the classroom. Check with the school's technology specialist to see what tools you have available.

- Podcasting and vodcasting are compatible with both PC and Mac. Podcasts usually require a microphone attached to a computer. Vodcasts require a camera to record the video. Some computers already have both of these functions built in which makes this type of media a quick reality.

- Make sure to test out the software and become familiar with it before introducing it into a lesson. Some students are very knowledgeable about video software and can teach you and/or serve as tutors to students in the class.

- Consult with the technology specialist to see how to upload these recordings to the school's webpage or class site. This will give parents and others the ability to access the information from outside of school.

Podcasting and Vodcasting Hints

There are many tutorials available online to help with this process. Check out different ways teachers have used podcasts and vodcasts in their classrooms as well. Simply type "podcasts in the classroom" into a search engine, and you may be amazed by what others are doing.

- Once you are acquainted with podcasting and vodcasting, video conferencing is just around the corner. Video conferencing is a great way to enhance instruction, deliver information, and bring in guest speakers.

- Incorporate musical talents. Instead of having students write and record a poem, let the students create a rap. Tailor the project to meet students' interests.

- Digital video can quickly turn into a vodcast if it is uploaded to the Internet and made available for others to download. This is a great way to share what students are learning and can be a learning tool for others. When students realize their final project may have a global audience, they may feel more empowered and dedicated to the project.

Preparing Students for Digital Media

School districts have guidelines and acceptable use policies (AUP) regarding the use of school and districtwide computer networks and the Internet. These terms and conditions identify acceptable online behavior and access privileges. Policies regarding the displaying of any student work must be adhered to strictly.

- Teach students safe, acceptable, and sensible behavior as online authors, readers, or producers.

- Inform parents of procedures and secure parental permission. Take the necessary steps to secure parental permission before using any online media for displaying student work.

- Review policies and guidelines pertaining to student access per your school or district.

- Teach students Internet safety; use the non-posting rules of no complete names, e-mail accounts, or references to reveal location.
- Set clear expectations regarding tone, respect, and consequences.

Preparing Your Classroom for Digital Media

You need to prepare your classroom for incorporating digital media. Depending on your space, you may want to designate an area for computers or technology. Post a list of student expectations while utilizing this space. To help students learn the technology, incorporate a word wall that lists all of the technological vocabulary related to the projects your students are working on.

Equipment and Funding

One of teachers' frequent complaints is inadequate equipment. Digital media does not require the most up-to-date computers and software, but it does need computers that can support the technology. Consult with your technology specialist or school media specialist to determine if your equipment is satisfactory or to find you the necessary equipment.

Funding is another problem often cited by educators who consider using digital media in the classroom. Find out if your school has a technology committee and get in contact with the committee that works with procuring a budget for different types of programs on campus. The more active and vocal you are about your needs, the more likely you are to get the equipment you want. In many schools funding is available for these types of programs.

You may also get funding by writing a grant. Grants are available every year for educators looking to incorporate new forms of technology in their classrooms. Start with an Internet search. Talk to other educators and people in your district to find out what grants your school or district has received in the past that may apply to you.

More Things to Consider

- Some blogs, podcasts, or vodcasts may be viewed publicly, as any other website. Educate and train students in privacy, security, and free expression.

- Most blogs have no editors. Be careful how you set up the blog and make sure to set clear expectations for students before beginning.

- Remind students to avoid content postings that could be interpreted as defamatory, libelous, or infringing upon the rights of others.

- Consult your school's administration before initiating any project that puts students in a public spotlight (such as posting videos to the Internet).

- Hardware or software issues could pose a potential problem.

- Students need to have access to computers that can run these types of Internet sites or software applications. Be aware of limitations and assign these types of projects accordingly.

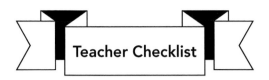

Teacher Checklist

Planning Research

Yes   No

☐   ☐   District policy is consulted before students post projects or comments online.

☐   ☐   Parents are made aware of the project and sign a consent form.

☐   ☐   Students are taught Internet safety precautions.

☐   ☐   You familiarize yourself with the software and create a sample project.

☐   ☐   You consult with a technology/media specialist to determine if you have the appropriate equipment.

☐   ☐   Digital media projects relate to objectives/standards.

☐   ☐   You engage the students in a lesson on how to use the hardware or software.

☐   ☐   You allow students creative control of their projects.

☐   ☐   Students know what qualities are expected of their project in order to demonstrate proficiency.

☐   ☐   You give students feedback on their projects.

☐   ☐   The physical arrangement of the classroom facilitates the technology projects.

☐   ☐   You model appropriate online behavior.

Yes   No

☐   ☐   Students clearly understand the assignment and what is expected of them.

☐   ☐   You consult with your school on how to post digital video to the website or classroom homepage.

APPLICATION

Feedback and Reflection

Feedback and Reflection — An Important Step in Learning

Feedback and reflection involves directing student learning by checking for understanding, giving student feedback, and/or encouraging student reflection. Many teachers become frustrated when they feel they have delivered an effective lesson and students perform very poorly on an assessment of their knowledge. Teachers can easily become wrapped up in teaching and assume that if students are in class and not disruptive, they are absorbing all that new knowledge from a teacher's passionate presentation.

To avoid disappointments in student achievement, an essential teaching responsibility is checking for understanding, giving students feedback, and stimulating reflection. Teachers need to ensure that students are grasping new concepts and knowledge. This does not mean simply posing the question, "Do you understand?" and continuing on with the lecture or presentation when one or two students nod their heads positively. Teachers need a more accurate assessment of student understanding.

Checking for Understanding

There are many different ways to check for understanding, some more formal than others. In this era of high-stakes testing, one of the most common forms of checking for understanding is having regular assessments that are closely aligned with final high-stakes tests or end-of-course exams. This type of checking for understanding is useful, particularly in subjects related to achievement on state tests. However, teachers of English language arts and mathematics should strive for levels of understanding beyond the low rigor/low relevance knowledge that is often required on state tests. Do not rely solely on common assessments to check for understanding. Some additional techniques to check for understanding include students' oral language, teacher questions, quick writes, projects and performances, and student body language (Fisher and Frey).

The practice of checking for understanding also includes formative assessment. A formative assessment is an assessment given during instruction. It allows teachers to make adjustments, leading to greater student understanding and achievement. In contrast, summative assessment is the final exam that a student takes at the completion of a course or year of study. Using common assessments and types of quizzes can be useful formative assessments during instruction.

Oral Language

Oral language is a dominant form of communication in the classroom. Teachers give oral directions and information. Teachers ask students to respond orally to questions and engage in discussion. When students use oral language, they expose their understanding of new material. Facilitate activities during lessons that allow students to use oral language. Monitor what students are saying as an informal measure of students' understanding of the content. To stimulate oral language, you can specifically ask students a question; however, a process that more fully engages the entire class is to facilitate student discussions either in pairs or small groups.

Another form of oral presentation used in checking for understanding is having students give oral summaries. For a further discussion of summarization, see the Summarization section in this handbook.

Using Oral Strategies to Check for Understanding

The following are several group activities. As a teacher listens to ideas or information shared by students, he or she can determine the level of understanding.

Compass Points. Students get into groups of four where each student is labeled north, south, east, or west. Ask students to reflect on a concept and draw a visual of his or her interpretation. The teacher then calls randomly on pairs of compass points to share with each other.

Circle, Triangle, Square. Have each student discuss the following: something that is still going around in your head (circle); something pointed that stood out in your mind (triangle); something that "squared" or agreed with your thinking (square).

Decisions, Decisions (Philosophical Chairs). Given a prompt, students go to the side of the room that corresponds to their opinion on the topic. Students share their reasoning for their beliefs and then are given the opportunity to change sides after discussion.

Example/Non-Example. Given a concept, students sort or write various examples and non-examples.

Reverse Example/Non-Example. Given examples and non-examples, students determine concept.

Fill in Your Thoughts. Students fill in the blank as a written check for understanding. (Another term for *rate of change* is _____ or _____ .)

Onion Ring. Students form an inner and outer circle facing a partner. The teacher asks a question, and the students are given time to respond to their partner. Next, the inner circle rotates one person to the left. The teacher asks another question, and the cycle repeats itself.

Say Something. In a cooperative group, students take turns leading discussions on sections of a reading or video.

Timed Pair Share. Given a prompt, students pair up and share their perspective for a set period of time.

Word Sort. Given a set of vocabulary terms, students sort them into given categories or create their own categories for sorting.

Whip Around. Teacher poses a question and asks students to write at least 3 items on a scrap of paper. When students have done so, they stand up, and the teacher randomly calls on one student to share one of the ideas from his or her paper. Students check off any items that are said by other students and sit down when all of the items have been shared within the class.

Using Questions

Questions are one of the most effective techniques to check for understanding. Ask higher-level questions to stimulate deeper understanding. If you only ask questions that require a simple recall answer, you do not know the students' depth of understanding. Without this deeper understanding, students are likely to forget information quickly.

One way to ensure full class participation when using teacher questions is to have some type of student response system. If you call on a single student and get the correct answer, you are only checking for understanding with one student, which may or may not reflect the understanding of the entire class. New technology applications have created a variety of electronic student response systems. These are excellent devices for posing questions to the entire class and require a response from every student. In this way, you can determine the level of understanding from everyone in the class.

In addition to high-tech solutions for audience response, you can create other forms of full-class response. Many teachers use small whiteboards with erasable markers that students can write an answer on and hold up for the teacher to see.

Using Writing to Check for Understanding

Using oral response is a good indication of understanding, but a more rigorous measure of depth of knowledge occurs when students are asked to write. The chapter "Writing to Learn" offers more thorough information on the use of student writing in the classroom. The following are several writing strategies:

Entrance/Exit Ticket. Each student is given a ticket to complete before leaving the room. The ticket may require students to answer one of the following questions: What is the most important thing I learned today? What questions do I still have? Students give these tickets to the teacher when exiting the room or upon entering the next day. The teacher uses this information to guide the instruction.

Give One, Get One. In this cooperative activity, students write responses to a prompt, meet up with another student, and share ideas so that each leaves with new thoughts to consider.

Take and Pass. This cooperative activity helps to share and collect information from each member of the group. Students write a response, pass their paper to the right, add their response to the next paper, and continue until they get their paper back. At the end the group debriefs.

Using Non-Verbal Checks for Understanding

Experienced teachers may not even need to ask a question in order to determine whether students are understanding concepts. Closely observing students and paying attention to verbal cues can provide a great deal of information on the level of student understanding. Watch for facial expressions, eye movement, or even restlessness to determine whether students are engaged and understanding the lesson. You can also develop a series of hand signals, such as thumbs up or thumbs down, for students to provide a reply. These quick body language signals are valuable but only work effectively in classrooms where teachers have established good relationships with students.

Another variation of non-verbal indicators is to incorporate physical movement. One way to do this is to gather feedback and actively engage students by setting up response areas in different parts of the room. Ask students to show degrees of agreement or disagreement to a particular question by physically moving to the corner of the room that represents their beliefs. Then invite students to discuss their opinions with others in that similar group and finally offer an opinion to the entire class. This physical movement is engaging for students and also provides a clear visual representation of what students are thinking. You can find additional information on this topic in the chapter on physical movement. The following are additional non-verbal activities you can use to check for understanding.

3-2-1/Fist to Five/Thumbs Up, Thumbs Down. Students communicate their level of understanding using their fingers.

4-3-2-1 Scoring Scale. This posted scale can either be used as a quick check with hand or a numerical value for students to self-assess a written assignment.

Every Pupil Response. Each student receives a pink and yellow card. Each color represents a specific response. Students raise the card to provide the correct response to a teacher-directed question.

Human Graph. In this kinesthetic activity, students in the class physically move to create a histogram. Students represent data points on the graph.

Interlocking Paper Plates. Students use two colored plates to provide feedback by sliding the two colored sections to show level of understanding.

Slap It. Teacher divides students into two teams to identify correct answers to questions given by the teacher. Students use a fly swatter to slap the correct response posted on the wall.

Triangular Prism (Red, Yellow, Green). Students give feedback to the teacher by displaying the color that corresponds to their level of understanding.

Using Projects and Performances to Check for Understanding

To achieve high rigor and relevance, consider student projects and performances as a way to demonstrate understanding. When students create projects, they must draw upon a greater depth of knowledge in order to complete the performance task. These types of measures only work well if the project or performance is directly related to the content learning. In addition, the project or performance must have a clear, high-quality scoring guide to evaluate student work.

Feedback

Feedback is connected to checking for understanding. When you become aware of the current level of student understanding through student responses or common assessments, you can stimulate student reflection by giving constructive feedback to students. Brookhart offers several suggestions for giving student feedback.

Timing is important. Feedback should occur as soon as possible after the teacher has assessed the current level of understanding. Also, the teacher should give essential feedback prior to a summative evaluation. This way the student has additional time to learn the required skills and knowledge.

Feedback should always be separate from comments about the individual student and focus exclusively on the quality of the work. Never label a student with a negative phrase such as "lazy," "careless," or "failing." These labels often discourage student effort because the student identifies with the label and feels that no amount of effort will achieve success. Likewise, labeling students as "good", "straight A" or "bright," can lead to problems. Again, students identify with the personal label and may not work as hard as they should. When they do not achieve, students may feel that the label is wrong. Keep all feedback about the work and not about the person.

Feedback should also be criterion referenced. Establish a specific scoring guide for performances and set clear expectations. Feedback should relate to the differences between student achievement and the expected criteria for effectiveness. Feedback should also be qualitative and provide enough specifics to give students ideas on how they can improve their performance. For example, in writing, the teacher should identify grammatical errors or weaknesses in tone or clarity to provide students helpful suggestions on how to improve their writing. In mathematics, the teacher should show the errors that students make in either interpreting the problem or constructing the solution. Always try to make feedback positive and encourage students to improve.

When giving oral feedback, make an attempt to provide feedback in a one-on-one conversation with the student. This can be done quietly at the student's desk while the rest of the class is working. You can also set up individual student conference times outside of class or after school. When significant negative feedback is necessary, be sure those conversations are in private. When positive feedback is appropriate to identify exemplary work, you may do this in front of the entire class to provide recognition. However, recognize that some students may be embarrassed by public accolades.

Reflection

Reflection is a quiet internal consideration of something. The word is from Latin -*flex* or bend, literally bending back. So reflection in learning is bending back and taking another look at what we have learned. Reflection is an important factor in learning. When students have the opportunity to reflect and are encouraged through some activity to reflect, it reinforces their learning and transfers new information into long-term memory. To prepare for application, students need to reflect on new information to store it in their brain and later retrieve it to connect with an application activity. When students reflect on new learning, they make the internal mental connections to retrieve that new knowledge at a later time.

You can initiate reflection among students in many different ways. A number of cooperative learning and group discussion techniques stimulate reflection. Teachers frequently use writing and journaling as reflection activities. Many checking-for-understanding activities described in this chapter stimulate important student reflection on a formative basis when students still have time to learn before being held accountable for applying the learning in a summative assessment.

Most importantly, allow time for students to reflect on their learning. Do not assume that just because students have heard or read information, they have retained it.

References

Brookhart, S., *How to Give Effective Feedback to Your Students*, Alexandria, Virginia: Association for Supervision and Curriculum Development, 2008

Fisher, D and Frey, N., *Checking for Understanding: Formative Assessment Techniques in Your Classroom*, Alexandria, Virginia: Association for Supervision and Curriculum Development, 2007

Resnick, L., O'Connor, C., and Michaels, S., *Classroom Discourse, Mathematical Rigor, and Student Reasoning: An Accountable Talk Literature Review*, 2007. Retrieved August 2010: www. learnlab.org/research/wiki/images/f/ff/Account-able_Talk_Lit_ Review.pdf

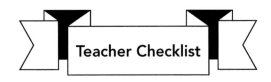

Teacher Checklist

Yes   No

☐   ☐   Time is taken frequently to check for understanding.

☐   ☐   Activities to check for understanding involve each student, not just a few.

☐   ☐   Activities to check for understanding frequently involve student movement.

☐   ☐   Students are shown and encouraged to listen deeply to other student conversation.

☐   ☐   Feedback is given on a timely basis.

☐   ☐   Feedback always focuses on the quality of the work and not the characteristics of the student.

☐   ☐   Feedback is positive and constructive.

☐   ☐   Feedback is criterion based.

☐   ☐   Feedback provides enough detail to enable students to improve their work.

☐   ☐   Students are encouraged to reflect on the quality of their work.

APPLICATION

Games

> Fun from games arises out of mastery. It arises out of the comprehension. It is the act of solving puzzles that makes games fun. In other words, with games, learning is the drug.
>
> — *Ralph Koster, A Theory of Fun*

Why We Enjoy Games

Games feed our mind just as food feeds our body. Brain chemicals, such as dopamine, give us a feeling of pleasure when released. We feel good. Games in which we are challenged to figure out a puzzle, better a previous score, or defeat another person give us feelings of euphoria because the brain release these pleasure enhancing chemicals.

Games can be played against other people, against you, against a computer, or perhaps even against the forces of nature. What they all have in common is that they have set goals with set rules that you have to follow in order to play. This makes it much easier for us to decide what to do and makes measuring the outcome simpler. We also have the learning aspect in games since in most games, we have to keep improving our skills in order to beat the competition (or our previous record). We naturally love games because success is easy to measure.

Games can be a learning strategy if used correctly with students. Games easily engage students because of this natural affinity we all have for them. A game as a strategy has some similarities to the strategy of play. The primary difference is that games always have clear structure and rules, whereas play is often unstructured and has few rules.

Why Use Games

- Makes learning fun
- Encourages classroom participation
- Encourages students to communicate with each other
- Breaks up the monotony of routine direct instruction
- Allows for learning in a low-stress environment

What Makes an Educational Game Successful?

Simplicity. Students need to quickly understand the games and the rules. Students should master the science, not the game itself.

Participation. All students must be able to be in the spotlight.

Goals. What is the objective of the game? The prize should be in the means, not the ends. The end result is knowledge.

Suspense. Students need to be curious.

Types of Games in the Classroom

Games can be divided into several categories. You can decide when and where to use these various types of games:

Memory Recall. Memory recall games are simple games where students recall specific facts or knowledge. Memory recall games are used to engage students in memorizing or practicing recall of knowledge. Games can be individual challenges like flashcards or team competition in classes for whole-group response. Memory recall can be used to reinforce essential knowledge or facts from a lecture or reading assignment. Examples include the following:

TV Game Shows. Numerous software and online versions of TV game shows, such as *Jeopardy!, Concentration, Pictionary, 21 Questions,* or *Taboo* are available to create computer slide presentations or interactive whiteboard applications easily.

Flashcards. You can make flashcards by writing on cardstock or using any of numerous online sites for using and/or creating flashcards.

Advantages
- Takes little time
- Can be customized to any content
- Offers high level of engagement

Disadvantages
- Emphasizes only low-rigor thinking

Resources
- Games for the Science Classroom: www.csun.edu/~vceed002/ref/games Downloadable game show templates
- SmartBoard Resources: www.bobsedulinks.com/Smart_Board_Links.htm
- Games for interactive whiteboards
- Fun Brain: www.funbrain.com Numerous recall games for all ages

Board Games

Board games involve the structure of game rules using a board as the focus of play. They usually include additional play pieces that provide questions, answers, and activities. Some board games are primarily for enjoyment among family and friends, but more and more board games are being created specifically for educational purposes. Examples include the following:

- Scrabble®
- Trivial Pursuit®
- Cranium
- Monopoly
- Apples to Apples®

Advantages
- Allows a complex learning experience that takes little preparation time by teacher
- May occupy extended periods of time

Disadvantages
- Are usually most engaging to younger students
- Must be stored and maintained for future use
- Are complex to create and usually cannot be customized

Resources
- 1888toys.com: www.1888toys.com
- Boardgame express: www.boardgameexpress.com

Simulation Games

Simulation games contain play objects, goals, and roles that reflect real-world objects and processes. Simulation provides a solution in education because so many of the things we need to understand these days are either too complex, too vast, too small, too far, or too dangerous to be experienced directly. Simulation is a fundamental educational tool to bring real-world experiences into the classroom. Simulation games can be either high fidelity or low fidelity. High-fidelity objects and processes are as close to reality as possible. Low-fidelity ones are based on simplified models of reality that incorporate only a few selected factors from the real world. Examples include the following:

- Sim City: http://simcity.ea.com

Advantages
- Are similar to the real world and offer effective transfer and application of knowledge
- Provide immediate and realistic feedback
- Allows you to make trial-and-error decisions and try what might be dangerous to do in the real world
- Allows for higher-order learning and in-depth analysis

Disadvantages
- Require a lot of time, work, and effort by both the teacher and the learners
- May be costs for software

Resources
- West Virginia Dept of Education Simulation Games: www.wv.gov/education/Pages/classroomsimulationgames.aspx
- University of Colorado Interactive Simulations: http://phet.colorado.edu
- ASPIRE Lab: http://sunshine.chpc.utah.edu/Civilization III: www.civ3.com/
- River City Project: http://muve.gse.harvard.edu/rivercityproject Environmental Detectives: http://education.mit.edu/ar/ed.html

Puzzles

Puzzles can be very engaging forms of games and can be used many different ways. You can use a puzzle as a bell-ringer activity for students to work on immediately upon entering a classroom. Having puzzles available can also keep students occupied (and out of trouble) when they have completed work faster than most of the other students. Word and math puzzles can be engaging ways for students to review vocabulary and math facts. Examples include the following:

- Word puzzles such as crosswords and anagrams
- Math puzzles such as Sudoku
- Jigsaw puzzles — Image might be a map in geography or works of art

Advantages
- Develops high-level thinking skills
- Allows students to work at their own pace
- Engages students and inspires many to stick with puzzle until it is solved

Disadvantages
- May frustrate struggling students
- May not always relate to standards

Resources
- Discovery Learning Puzzle Maker: http://puzzlemaker.discoveryeducation.com
- Crossword Puzzle Games: www.crosswordpuzzlegames.com/create.html
- Tools for Educators: www.toolsforeducators.com
- Anagram Genius: www.anagramgenius.com
- Word Search Maker: www.greyolltwit.com/wsearch.html
- Math Puzzle: www.mathpuzzle.com
- Teachnology: www.teach-nology.com/printables/puzzles

Multi-Sensory Games

This is the category that most people refer to as video games. Games are played on a computer or game device connected to a video display. Games have the structure of rules, and players compete against other players or seek to beat a previous best score. Games have multiple levels that increase in difficulty as the game proceeds. Usually the game requires eye-hand coordination as well as making cognitive choices. Games create simulated and sometimes very realistic environments. Multi-sensory games have become so sophisticated they are used in military and public safety training. Multi-sensory games are very engaging since they create high levels of common game characteristics: high levels of user control, immediate feedback, ever increasing challenge, multi-sensory involvement that requires full concentration, and blocking out environment. Examples include the following:

- Quest Atlantis: http://atlantis.crlt.indiana.edu
- Re-Mission: www.re-mission.net

Advantages
- Are highly engaging

Disadvantages
- Require technology investment
- May frustrate struggling students
- May not have high educational value

Resources
- Academic Skill Builders: www.arcademicskillbuilders.com DimensionU games from Tabula Digital: www.dimension.com Institute of Play: www.instituteofplay.com
- Leap Frog Games: http://shop.leapfrog.com/leapfrog Scholastic Games: www.scholastic.com/parents/play/games

Icebreakers

Icebreakers can be used to help students get to know one another and for you to get to know students. Icebreakers help students clear their attention to previous classes and events in their personal lives and prepare them for focusing on a daily class. Some icebreakers can be directly tied to the content of a lesson and used to generate interest in a topic. For example, you may do an inventory of eye color prior to introducing a lesson on genetics. Icebreakers, when related to the lesson topic, can be used to determine student's prior knowledge. Examples include the following:

Alike and Different. Randomly assign students to pairs. Give student pairs two minutes to see who can list the most items in common (number of siblings, street they live on, favorite sport, favorite meal). Give a small prize to the winning team. As an option, you can repeat this with one or two additional pairs. Then have pairs of students note differences. Ask that they not use physical appearance characteristics. Finally, ask students to reflect on the many similarities and differences among all people.

People Bingo. Create a Bingo card with 25 squares. Tell students to put their names in the center square. Put a question in each of the other squares. Questions may include: Who has a younger sister? Who has traveled outside of the United States? Who was born in a different state? Have students search for people who meet the criterion of the question and write the name in the square. Give a prize to the first person who has answers to five questions horizontally, vertically, or diagonally.

Ball Toss. Arrange students in a circle along with yourself. Explain that you are going to say your name and throw a ball to someone. The person that catches the ball then says, "Thanks {insert teacher name}, my name is {insert name}." The student then tosses the ball to someone else. The ball continues to be tossed until everyone has been introduced. Once everyone has been introduced, you can have students call out a name before they toss the ball to reinforce student names.

The Story of Your Name. Ask students to turn to a partner and explain what their name means and where it comes from (if they know). Most students reveal a surprising amount of interesting information. After partners have worked together, ask each student to introduce his/her partner to the larger group and explain what his/her name means and where it comes from. The greater the ethnic and cultural diversity in the group, the better this exercise tends to work.

Get with the Beat. Assemble students into a big circle. Say your name with a motion for each syllable. The entire group then says your name with the motions. The next person says his/her name with a motion for each syllable. The entire group says your name with the motions and then the second person's name with the motions to repeat all names. Continue around the circle.

Balloon Toss. Have each student answer these three questions on a small sheet of paper.

- What is something personal about you that people do not know?
- What is something you are proud of?
- What is something peculiar about you?

Have students roll the paper small enough to fit in a balloon. Have students blow up and tie off balloons with their note inside. Have students toss balloons in the air and keep all balloons aloft. After a minute, have each student grab a balloon, pop it, and remove the paper. Each student tries to find the student who wrote the answers.

People Puzzle. Rather than just assigning groups when forming teams, make it fun to discover partners. Create (or download) a puzzle with the same number of pieces as there will be students on a team. Cut the pieces and distribute them to the class. Ask students to find their partners by matching pieces.

Advantages
- Low cost
- Easy to set up
- Highly engaging

Disadvantages
- Not always related directly to instruction

Resources
- Group-game.com: www.group-games.com/games-by-type
- Icebreakers, Fun Games, Group Activities: www.icebreakers.ws
- Teacher Vision: www.teachervision.fen.com/icebreaker/resource/6063.html
- Mike Wills Icebreaker Collection: www.mwls.co.uk/icebreakers

References

Csíkszentmihályi, M. *Flow: The Psychology of Optimal Experience.* New York: Harper and Row. 1990

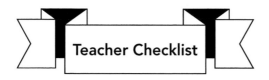

Teacher Checklist

Yes	No	
☐	☐	Purpose of the game is clear to teacher.
☐	☐	Purpose of the game is clear to students.
☐	☐	All students are able to participate in some manner.
☐	☐	Students have equal chance to participate.
☐	☐	Rules of the game are clear to students.
☐	☐	Students reflect on the game after playing.
☐	☐	All materials necessary for the game are available.
☐	☐	The right amount of time is allotted to the game.
☐	☐	Students are actively engaged.
☐	☐	The game is appropriately challenging to students.
☐	☐	If the game is not working, changes are made or the game is abandoned.
☐	☐	The game avoids embarrassing or devaluing any students.

K
N
O
W
L
E
D
G
E

APPLICATION

Instructional Technology— Any Time

What Does "Any Time" Mean?

Instructional technology adds more options to a teacher's collection of strategies. Technology is a highly engaging strategy for students. "Any time" refers to various technology applications that break the barriers of students in a single class for a specific amount of time. Students learn outside the class period and classroom. This strategy uses Internet-connected digital technology — blogs, microblogs, virtual communities, wikis, and online lectures — for asynchronous interactive learning.

Online Etiquette

Students working in an online environment means the teacher is not visibly present to monitor students' activity. However, students should still follow certain rules. Online communication presents students with the challenge of overcoming a lack of non-verbal cues in communication. Remind students of several points of etiquette.

1. **Avoid language that may come across as strong or offensive.** Language can be easily misinterpreted in short written communication. If a point must be stressed, review the statement to make sure that outsiders reading it will not be offended. Humor and sarcasm may easily be misinterpreted as well, so try to be as matter-of-fact and professional as possible.

2. **Keep writing to the point and stay on topic.** Online instruction requires a lot of reading. When writing, keep sentences poignant and brief so that readers do not get lost in wordy paragraphs and miss the point of the statement. Also, be careful about introducing new topics; it may confuse others.

3. **Read first, write later.** Read all posts or comments of other discussions before personally commenting to prevent repeating commentary or asking questions that have already been answered.

4. **Think before you push the send button**. Did you write what you meant? There's no taking back a sent comment, so double check all writing to make sure that it clearly conveys the exact intended message.

5. **An online classroom is still a classroom**. Appropriate classroom behavior is still mandatory. Respect for fellow classmates and the teacher is as important. Any derogatory or inappropriate comments regarding race, gender, age, religion, and sexual orientation are unacceptable and subject to the same disciplinary action that they would receive if they occurred in the physical classroom.

6. **Do not harass or offend.** Encourage an environment of respect and kindness in all digital communications in the online classroom and the larger global community.

7. **Use the language of the Internet.** Though still a fairly young type of communication, certain aspects of this form of communication are becoming conventional. For example, do not write using all capital letters because it appears as shouting. Also, the use of emoticons, such as :-) or :-(, can be helpful when conveying non-verbal feelings. However, avoid overusing them.

8. **Watch your writing style.** Publishing is not the same as texting or email. Informal abbreviations and language, such as "CU L8R" or "I'll send it 2 U", should be avoided.

9. **Consider privacy and rights of others.** Ask permission prior to giving out a classmate's email address or other information. Seek permission before using photos or videos of others. Be sure to properly cite all resources used and to give appropriate credit to authors and sources.

10. **If possible, keep attachments small.** If it is necessary to send pictures, change the size to an acceptable 100K. Reduce the size of photos, video, and graphics.

11. **Do not use inappropriate material.** Do not forward virus warnings, chain letters, or jokes to classmates or instructors. The sharing of pornographic material is forbidden.

Any Time Instructional Uses

- *Student discussion* — Teachers post questions online for student to engage in blog discussions.

- *Feedback and review* — Students read the work of another student and comment on the blog.

- *Cooperative learning* — Students contribute to a discussion in order to add depth or solve problems.

- *Summarizing experiences and conveying meaning* — Students summarize key facts of their learning.

- *Research and inquiry* — Students research a topic, summarize results, include links, and reflect on their findings.

- *Critical thinking* — Using threaded discussions, students analyze and critically think on issues and topics.
- *Presentation/exhibition* — Students express ideas using a variety of digital formats.
- *Web-based learning* — Students connect to a wide range of online resources to support learning.
- *Collaborative learning* — Students co-create a collection of online resources for learning.
- *Storytelling* — Students share images or other media to represent experiences, viewpoint, and meaning.

Students can contribute solutions and solve problems as determined by you.

Classroom Blogging

The term *blog* is short for *weblog* and is defined as an online journal or diary. Blogs are an excellent tool for supporting both the reading and writing process. With a blog, any individual can publish work online. Blog settings allow for work to be published locally to a single class or to a larger global audience. Posts can also be closed and available only to those given a link or entry. The open nature of the publishing and comments creates a conversation around the topics being discussed. For many students, seeing work published online can be a motivator. A variety of blogging tools exist, and many of these tools are free.

Blogging Suggestions
- Decide how blogging can best support your curriculum and which instructional strategies to use in the blogging process.
- Discuss online etiquette with students to encourage responsible and appropriate use.
- Know your school's Acceptable Use Policy for Technology.
- Get parental permission, if necessary according to your school or district policy.

- View terms of service of the blogging tool selected, including age limits and other rules put in place by the provider. Remind students to view these terms of service on any online site they use and to avoid giving personal information.

- Become an administrator for your class blogs, if possible. Learn how to moderate comments as needed.

- Allow students to view other student/teacher blogs before working with the class blogs.

- Model the technology that you wish students to use. For example, use a blog to post assignments or share reflections.

- Give students a list of what should be included in their blog and the content which is being addressed.

- Teach students how to comment on blog posts and tell them what their comments should include.

Blogging Resources

Index of Award Winning Education Blogs: http://edublogawards.com

List of Education Blogs from Will Richardson: http://supportblogging.com/Links+to+School+Bloggers

Blogging Tools

- Edublogs: http://edublogs.org
- Blogger: www.blogger.com
- Kidblog: http://kidblog.org/home.php
- Wordpress: http://wordpress.com

Using Virtual Communities

Social networking sites such as Facebook and Myspace are popular with students. Social networks have been described as web-based services that allow people to (Boyd and Ellison):

- Construct a public or semi-public profile within a bounded system
- Articulate a list of other users with whom they share a connection
- View and traverse their list of connections and those made by others within the system

The nature and nomenclature of these connections may vary from site to site. There is limited value in school for true social networking sites. However, similar network sites can be used as virtual communities.

Virtual communities exist online to connect individuals with common interests and goals. In classrooms, creating a virtual community space gives teachers and students an online venue for student sharing, connecting, and discussion. In addition, it gives an opportunity to practice digital skills through the various tools found within the virtual community/social networking tool: threaded discussions, creation of like groups, link sharing, photo and video sharing, and more.

On many social networking sites, the student has a page for posting and customizing that allows one-to-one and one-to-many interactions. This enhances creativity, communication, and collaboration. The easy, interactive nature of the tools aids student interaction and learning and provides motivation. Many varieties of social networking and virtual community tools are available that can be used in the classroom. Some are pay based, and some are free.

Virtual Community Suggestions

- Decide how virtual online communities/social network sites can best support your curriculum and select strategies that will enhance this use.
- Join a social network for teachers to become familiar with the styles of communication used and to practice with the tools.
- Discuss online etiquette with students to encourage responsible and appropriate use.
- Know your school's Acceptable Use Policy for Technology.

- Get parental permission, if necessary according to your school or district policy.

- View terms of service for the tool selected, including age limits and other rules for the site put in place by the provider. Remind students to view these terms of service on any online tool they use and to avoid giving personal information.

- Model the technology that you wish the students to use. For example, demonstrate uses and originate posts of varying styles and formats.

- Give all students a clear idea of what type of content should be included.

- Teach students how to reply to threaded discussions, how to post images and videos, and how to customize their own profile page.

- Teach students how to post links to online sources within posts and throughout the site.

- Teach students how to create groups or lists of followers to allow for quick collaboration and quality content distribution on the site.

Virtual Community Site Resources
- Educators Ning: http://edupln.ning.com
- Classroom 2.0: www.classroom20.com

Virtual Community Site Tools
- Grouply: www.grouply.com
- GROU.PS: http://grou.ps
- Ning: www.ning.com

Using Microblogs in the Classroom

Microblogging is an abbreviated form of blogging. In microblogging, posts are brief and consist of a limited number of letters, numbers, or characters. With one popular microblog, Twitter, posts are comprised of

140 characters or less. Microblogging can be used both synchronously and asynchronously.

Microblogs are an easy way to publish information online. Microblogging privacy settings allow for work to be published either publicly or to only a selected online group. Additionally, using microblog search tools, you can easily search conversations and posts according to keyword.

Collaboration via microblogging is easy. These tools can engage a few students, a whole classroom, and even people outside of your classroom. Communication is facilitated in microblogging because of the means of searching and collating results. The ease of use and the ability to get responses quickly can be a great motivator for students. Microblogging is popular because it can be done from mobile phones virtually anywhere. A variety of micoblogging tools exist, and many of these tools are free.

Microblogging Suggestions

- Decide how microblogging can best support your curriculum and select strategies that will enhance this use.

- Discuss online etiquette with students to encourage responsible and appropriate use.

- Know your school's Acceptable Use Policy for Technology.

- Get parental permission, if necessary according to your school or district policy.

- Microblog services are a form of social networking. View terms of service of the microblogging tool selected, including age limits and other rules put in place by the provider. Remind students to view these terms of service on any online tool they use and to avoid giving personal information.

- Allow students to see how Twitter/microblogging is used.

- Model the technology that you wish the students to use. For example, demonstrate uses and give examples of future use.

- Give all students a clear idea of what type of content should be included.
- Teach students how to reply and retweet or share content from microblogging or Twitter sites.
- Teach students how to use microblogging search mechanisms such as hashtags for easy searching of information and content.
- Teach students how to create groups or lists of followers to allow for quick collaboration and quality content.

Microblogging Resources
- Hashtags for Education by Jerry Blumengarten: www.cybrary-man.com/edhashtags.html
- Directory of Educators on Twitter: http://twitter4teachers.pb-works.com

Microblogging Tools
- Twitter: www.twitter.com
- Posterous: www.posterous.com
- Edmodo: www.edmodo.com
- Plurk: www.plurk.com

Wikis in the Classroom

The term *wiki* originates from the Hawaiian word *wiki* meaning quick. A wiki is an online space for posting any content such as text, video, and audio. Wikis are constructed to allow multiple persons to sign in and edit content. Anyone given access to a wiki can generally edit any content. The best known wiki is Wikipedia, an online free encyclopedia. Contribution update history is contained in the wiki; therefore, you can easily see who and when contributions are made. Wikis can be used in the classroom to support a number of instructional strategies and are especially well suited for student collaboration and interaction.

Wiki Suggestions

- Decide what instructional strategies you will focus on most by using wikis.

- View various types of classroom wikis and see the various types of projects completed by other classrooms.

- Discuss online etiquette with students to encourage responsible and appropriate use.

- Know your school's Acceptable Use Policy for Technology.

- Get parental permission, if necessary according to your school or district policy.

- View terms of service of the wiki tool selected, including age limits and other rules put in place by the provider. Remind students to view these terms of service on any online site they use and to avoid giving personal information.

- Set up the wiki, decide level of public view, and determine how you will moderate participation.

- Discuss how wikis work with students. Have them view and analyze Wikipedia, a large-scale wiki for public contribution. Allow students to view other wikis that have been created by other classrooms.

- Model the technology that you wish the students to use. For example, use a wiki to create classroom content and share links with students.

- Give students a list of what they are expected to contribute. What are the common objectives? Tell students how their contributions will be assessed. Make sure they know how the end product should look.

- Teach students how to use the discussion board feature.

- Teach students how to use revision history.

Wiki Resources

- Digitally Speaking Wiki Resource by Bill Ferriter: http://digitallyspeaking.pbworks.com/Wikis
- Flat Classroom Project: http://flatclassroomproject.wikispaces.com
- List of Educational Wikis: http://educationalwikis.wikispaces.com/ Examples of educational wikis

Wiki Tools

- Wikispaces: www.wikispaces.com
- PBWiki: www.pbwiki.com

Online Lectures — Podcasts and Video Lectures

The traditional classroom has lecture as a standard component. The modern classroom recognizes that learning can occur any time of day and inside or outside the classroom. Teachers in the 21st-century classroom know that a wide array of available online content supports school curriculum and standards. Listening to podcasts and watching video lectures helps students learn and fosters independent learning. Some classrooms are flipping the activities typically seen as classroom activities and homework activities. Lecture learning is now done independently by the student, and classroom time is reserved for project and real-world learning. Refer to the Video strategy for sources and suggestions for video as online lectures.

Traditional Lecture	21st-Century Lecture
In classroom	Online
Given by teacher only	Accessed from a variety of educational and professional sources
Given only once and is non-recurring	Can be revisited and accessed repeatedly as needed for reinforcement
Accessed only during class	Can be accessed 24 hours a day/7 days a week
Uses a large percentage of class time	When done independently by students, can free up class time for hands on, real-world projects

Examples

- Lit2Go: http://etc.usf.edu/lit2go
- iTunes University: www.apple.com/education/itunes-u Access via iTunes
- Stanford University (university providing lecture and video content): http://itunes.stanford.edu

References

Boyd, D. & N. Ellison, "Social network sites: Definition, History, and Scholarship." *Journal of Computer-Mediated Communication*, 13(1), article 11. 2007. Retrieved August 2010:http://jcmc. indiana.edu/vol13/issue1/boyd.ellison.html.

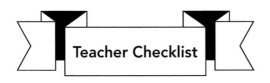

Teacher Checklist

Yes   No

☐   ☐   Selected objectives and strategies are supported by the technology application.

☐   ☐   Students are told what types of reflection to include in their online writing.

☐   ☐   Students know exactly what is expected.

☐   ☐   Students are shown or know how to access online tools/ content.

☐   ☐   Online tools are checked public or private, as appropriate.

☐   ☐   Students know how to use the features of the microblog, virtual community, wiki, or online lecture.

☐   ☐   Students know the rules of online etiquette, responsible posting, and citation of sources.

☐   ☐   Students know exactly how they are going to be assessed.

☐   ☐   Students can easily access content.

K
N
O
W
L
E
D
G
E

APPLICATION

Instructional Technology— Real Time

What Does "Real Time" Mean?

Instructional technology adds more options to a teacher's collection of strategies. Technology is a highly engaging strategy for students. "Real time" refers to various applications that teachers and students use within the regular class period to enhance learning. This strategy uses Internet-connected digital technology for group instruction, including interactive whiteboards, computers, and portable devices. Synchronous uses of technology are mentioned here. In these uses, shared access to the technology occurs at the same time by more than one person. In some cases, responses and feedback are instantaneous and, therefore, synchronous.

Real-Time Technology Instructional Uses

Presentations/Exhibitions. Students present and organize information relevant to their learning. They also get real-world experience with communication skills.

Service Learning. Students connect to other students and professionals globally both to learn and add value to the community.

Socratic Seminar. Students respond to questions and teacher inquiry though online connections.

Teaching Others. Students deepen knowledge by teaching other students and from peer interaction.

Storytelling. Students share their ideas and concepts with others and share video, photos, and links.

Lecture. Students learn by listening to an online lecture and getting links and materials related to the learning.

Feedback and Review. Students read the work of another student and comment online.

Cooperative Learning. Students contribute to a discussion in order to add depth or solve problems.

Problem-based Learning. Students investigate solutions and share resources and solutions.

Summarizing Experiences and Conveying Meaning. Students summarize facts discovered.

Research and Inquiry. Students quickly find needed information.

Artistic Expression. Both teachers and students create visual displays to express thoughts, ideas, concepts and meaning.

Summarizing Experiences and Conveying Meaning. Both teachers and students use and create content using the interactive whiteboard to summarize key facts of their learning.

Digital Media Production. Teachers and students create content to express ideas, thoughts, and concepts. They can include audio, images, video, and other content to explain meaning and share with classmates or post online.

Guided Practice. Teachers and students use the interactive board for problem solving and reinforcement of concepts and skills.

Using Skype in the Classroom

Skype is a tool for video and online chatting. Skype uses VOIP (voice over Internet protocol) and allows for easy and quick online connections. Skype settings allow for teachers and administrators to communicate easily with other educators. It is a collaborative tool that can include conversation and instruction from people outside of your classroom to enhance the learning process and engage students.

Skype Suggestions

- Explore new communication methods for accomplishing learning tasks.
- Discuss online etiquette with students to encourage responsible and appropriate use.
- Know your school's Acceptable Use Policy for Technology.
- Get parental permission, if necessary according to your school or district policy.
- Test the software, the camera, and the microphone that you are using in advance of class sessions to ensure proper functioning.
- Explore the features of the program used.
- Plan online sessions in advance to optimize use of learning time.
- Allow students to practice using Skype and its features.
- Give students a list of the objectives of the online session.
- Look at sample Skype projects before planning your own.

Skype Resources

- Technology 4 Kids Skype Resources: http://technology4kids.pbworks.com/Skype
- Skype in School Wiki: http://skypeinschools.pbworks.com
- Skype Around the World (by Silvia Tolisano): http://langwitches.org/blog/2009/12/16/k12online09
- Skype: www.skype.com

21 Ways to Use Skype in the 21st-Century Classroom

- Interview an author.
- Speak with a professional on the job.
- Visit with another classroom in your district.
- Visit with a classroom in another state or country.
- Present student work.
- Take a virtual field trip to another country.
- Visit a museum virtually.
- Learn a new language.
- Gain a new skill.
- Teach a skill to others.
- Start a student homework help desk.
- Allow sick or at-home students to attend class.
- Take professional development.
- Deliver professional development.
- Collaborate with other teachers.
- Find a mentor teacher.
- Take a class online.
- Share student work with parents.
- Connect with grandparents.
- Conduct parent conferences.
- Collect and share images and videos from Skype calls.

Using Cell Phones in the Classroom

Today's cell phones have many capabilities that have expanded their benefits and relevance to the everyday classroom. They are readily accessible and easily portable. The relatively low cost makes them an equitable tool as many students already have access to cell phones. Using cell phones creates a real-world environment where students can learn and apply new skills easily. Classroom management techniques support active engagement and successful instructional use. Cell phones have calling capability and other functions such as texting and calculator. Currently, the term *smartphone* refers to any cell phone that also has the additional enhancement of full-Internet capability.

Cell Phone Suggestions

- Decide how cell phone use can best support your curriculum and which instructional strategies to use.
- Discuss cell phone etiquette with students to encourage responsible and appropriate use.
- Have rules for cell phones that include when and in what circumstances phones can be used.
- Know your school's Acceptable Use Policy for Technology.
- Get parental permission, if necessary according to school or district policy. Be specific about tasks students will be involved in.

Sample Cell Phone Lessons

Research and Inquiry. Students search for details on a news story. Results can be sent via text to students who can add facts to a classroom wiki. Results can include links, images, videos, and audio content.

Feedback and reflection. Use the classroom polling feature to ascertain student understanding of a classroom topic. Give the link to students so that they can respond to the poll. You can pull up the poll results and determine next steps according to results.

Cooperative Learning. Students search for images and details about the location for an upcoming field trip. They can add these facts and images to a shared website to enhance knowledge of the location and types of experiences they might have.

Resources for Using Cell Phones in the Classroom

- Mobile Devices in the Classroom Article-District Administrator: www.districtadministration.com/viewarticle.aspx?articleid=2198
- PEW Study on Use of Cell Phones in Young: http://pewresearch.org/pubs/1572/teens-cell-phones-text-messages
- Learning in Hand: http://learninginhand.com/blog/tag/video
- Innovative Educator Blog: New Technology and Ideas for Using Cell Phones in Schools: http://theinnovativeeducator.blogspot.com

Instructional Strategy	Cell Phone Technology
Cooperative learning	Texting
Problem-based learning	Microblogging/Twitter
Research and inquiry	Networking tools
Summarization and meaning conveyance	Software applications
	Internet search
Presentation and real-world communication skills	Data collection
	GPS — Global Positioning System
	Camera
	Video camera
	Bluetooth connectivity
	Headsets
	Audio and music capabilities
	File storage
	Capabilities will continue to expand

Interactive Whiteboards in the Classroom

Many classrooms today have installed interactive whiteboards to enhance delivery and instruction. Many different types of interactive whiteboards are made by a variety of manufacturers. A salient feature of the interactive boards is the ability for touch interaction on the large viewing screen. This allows creating and manipulating images and text. As both teachers and students can interact with these whiteboards, the technology greatly contributes to an engaging classroom environment. Many varieties of interactive whiteboards also come with software made especially for the educational environment. This software often contains templates and images suited to each curriculum area and applicable to many grade levels. In addition, individual lesson plans to use on the boards exist on manufacturer websites and are frequently shared by educators in many locations online.

A whiteboard's large viewing area and positioning lends itself to classroomwide engagement and access. Viewing Internet websites and exploring content is easier for the whole class. The instructional use of the board makes it a valuable classroom tool. Student involvement and interaction expands the benefit.

Interactive Whiteboard Suggestions

- Decide how the interactive board can support your curriculum and which instructional strategies to use.
- Discuss proper care of the board.
- Learn what you need to know about the technical setup of the board.
- Install the current version of the software on your computer.
- Install the software on any home or personal computer you have so that you can practice and plan lessons.
- Explore and practice with the features of the board to gain familiarity before using it for a lesson.
- Explore the curriculum tools available in the software found with the board.
- Explore the many sites online for use on the interactive board.
- If the board is shared among other classes, be sure that you have access to the interactive board when your class needs it.
- Allow students to explore and practice with the features of the board before using it for a classroom lesson.
- Model the technology that you wish the students to use. Be open to using the board in new ways for instruction.
- Give students guidelines for what contributions they will make when working on the interactive whiteboard.

Resources for Using Interactive Whiteboards

- Educational Leadership — Robert Marzano on Smartboard Use: www.ascd.org/publications/educational-leadership/nov09/vol67/num03/Teaching-with-Interactive-Whiteboards.aspx
- Interactive Whiteboard Virtual Community for Teachers — Smartboard Revolution: http://smartboardrevolution.ning.com
- Smart Exchange Lesson Plans: http://exchange.smarttech.com/#tab=0
- Lessons Podcasts by Ben Hazzard: www.podcastdirectory.com/podcasts/11896
- Collection of Interactive Sites: www.internet4classrooms.com/links_grades_kindergarten_12/whiteboard_interactive_site.htm
- Teacher Tap Interactive Websites: http://eduscapes.com/tap/topic86.htm
- National Library of Math Manipulatives: http://nlvm.usu.edu/en/nav/vlibrary.html

Web Browsing

Web browsing is the act of looking through and searching information contained on the Internet. Resources are located through a URL, or uniform resource locator. This gives a unique and distinct location to the content contained. The Internet acts as a very large database, and information contained there is constantly growing and changing. New formats for browsing are invented daily, providing a seemingly limitless treasure trove of information. This information is invaluable to the classroom and provides an excellent platform for search, inquiry, and collaboration. Efficient means and resources for using the Internet exist for educational purposes. Search engines are incredibly powerful and convenient for locating information. Using these resources in instruction can open up a world of learning to students.

Web Browsing References

- Wikipedia: http://en.wikipedia.org/wiki/Web_browser
- Finding Dulcinea: www.findingdulcinea.com/guides.topic_s_categories_ss_guide-to-web-search.xa_1.html

Web Browsing Suggestions

- Emphasize information literacy and proper use of available content.

- Explore new communication methods for accomplishing learning tasks.

- Discuss online etiquette with students to encourage responsible and appropriate use.

- Know your school's Acceptable Use Policy for Technology.

- Give students a list of the objectives of the online session.

- Teach website evaluation for sources. Help students learn to critically evaluate content for author, date, intent, and bias.

- Communicate educational goals and assessment strategies.

- Get parental permission, if necessary according to school or district policy.

- Test the software to ensure proper functionality.

- Explore the features of the browser.

- Plan online sessions in advance to optimize use of learning searches.

- Use quality sources such as primary sources.

- Check to make sure students can access sites though the school filtering system. Use the local procedures for making sure students have access to educational sites.

Web Browsing Resources

- Learn about Web Browsers: www.whatbrowser.org/en

- Ten Steps for Better Web Searching: www.sweetsearch.com/TenSteps

- Internet Public Library: www.ipl.org

- Fact Monster: www.factmonster.com

- Federal Resources for Educational Excellence (Free primary sources and more): http://free.ed.gov

- Library of Congress: www.loc.gov/index.html
- Safe Searches for Young Students: www.sldirectory.com/searchf/kidsafe.html
- KidsClick — Search Sites by Librarians: www.kidsclick.org
- Sweet Search — Search Engine for Students: www.sweetsearch.com

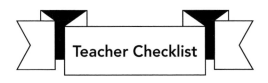

Teacher Checklist

Yes   No

☐   ☐   Technology activities are related to learning objectives.

☐   ☐   Students are told what types of interaction they should contribute.

☐   ☐   Students are shown or know how to use the tools and software.

☐   ☐   Students follow the rules of online etiquette and responsible posting.

☐   ☐   Appropriate permissions are in place, and the AUP permissions are in place.

☐   ☐   Classroom management strategies guide students in how and when technology will be used.

☐   ☐   Students know how to use the technology features, such as taking photos or videos and sharing content.

☐   ☐   You are familiar with the website for the interactive whiteboard and explored other sites with lesson plans for use.

☐   ☐   Students know exactly what is expected when technology is used in classroom activities.

☐   ☐   Students use technology along with you.

☐   ☐   Students know how to use the features of the interactive whiteboard, such as using the pens and inserting photos, clipart, images, and multimedia.

Yes	No	
☐	☐	Students know and follow rules for online posting of content created on the whiteboard.
☐	☐	Students know how to evaluate for quality resources.
☐	☐	Students know what should be created or published as a result of Internet searching.
☐	☐	Students know how their work will be assessed.
☐	☐	Students know how to save websites for later use.
☐	☐	Students know how to cite resources properly.
☐	☐	Students know how to use advanced search techniques, if appropriate.

APPLICATION

Learning Centers

What Are Learning Centers?

Learning centers are areas set up around a classroom for brief student activities that focus on developing a particular skill and/or concept. Students may work individually or in cooperative groups. The term *learning centers* can mean different things to different educators. Two other terms are often used interchangeably with learning centers: *literacy centers* and *learning stations*.

The most frequent definition of learning centers, and one of the earliest uses of the term, comes from the National Association for the Education of Young Children (NAEYC). It defines learning centers as "areas/activities that allow children to manipulate materials; explore ideas; discover consequences; build, create, and express themselves through art mediums. Learning centers give the child an opportunity to make decisions and choose the timing of his or her learning." This While this vision gives the student opportunity to make decisions, other educators may use learning centers a little differently.

A literacy center is common in elementary schools, where learning centers are used frequently and the focus is on literacy.

Literacy centers are considered the same as learning centers, with the understanding that the focus is exclusively on literacy: reading, writing and listening.

A learning station is teacher directed and more sequential as students work to move through the stations. Many educators distinguish between learning centers and learning stations by the purpose of these locations in the classroom. In this chapter, we will use the single term *learning centers* but with slightly different purposes and applications.

Some may have the perception that learning centers are only for younger children or that they are set up only for free-time for unstructured academic practice. Certainly those scenarios exist. However, learners achieve well in learning centers because of the student-centered and independent inquiry approach. More importantly, students are more satisfied and confident in their ability to learn. Learning centers can be an effective strategy in many different classrooms and at different levels.

Optional Uses of Learning Centers

To encompass all of the variations of learning centers, literacy centers and learning stations, the following list explains how some types of learning centers can be used in various classroom settings.

Learning centers for inquiry and exploration — This highly student-centered approach is recommended for early childhood education. The teacher creates optional centers with rich and diverse materials that allow students to choose to play and explore learning. In these types of learning centers, students choose where they will spend their time.

Learning centers for literacy centers — In primary grades, literacy centers provide differentiated student-centered learning exclusively focused on literacy skills. In literacy centers, students might have some unstructured choices similar to inquiry and exploration, but teachers might encourage participation in selected centers depending on the needs of the students.

Learning centers for differentiated instruction — One of the strategies to differentiate instruction is to create learning centers where students have greater flexibility of time or student work to develop learning outcomes. Teachers might design different centers to specifically reach different learning styles. Teachers assign or direct the movement of students based upon individual learning needs.

Learning centers for developing independent engaged learners — In these centers, teachers focus on creating multiple modalities of learning related to a common theme. For example, an elementary classroom might select a theme of whales. In different stations, students might read a book on whales, view a video, calculate sizes of different whales, draw a whale, write an imaginative narrative about a whale seeing a ship, or research and diagram the migration of a whale species. Students rotate among the centers, eventually completing all tasks.

Learning centers for sequential student-centered learning — In these types of centers, the teacher breaks a student performance into several sequential steps. Students move through the steps/centers at their own pace to eventually complete the total performance. Using sequential centers or stations differentiates time for student learning. Students that need more time to write or read at one of the centers have more time. These centers also help to more efficiently use limited instructional resources and equipment.

Benefits of Learning Centers

Regardless of the type and purpose of a learning center, it provides many benefits. Learning centers do the following:

- Provide opportunities for students to explore, discover, create, practice, and apply skills
- Promote critical and creative thinking skills
- Stimulate cooperative learning
- Address different learning styles when a variety of activities are available for student choice
- Allow the teacher opportunities for flexible grouping and varied activities such as individual conferencing and guided reading groups

- Promote independent learning
- Provide opportunities for students to take responsibility for their learning and demonstrate what they have learned

Learning Centers for Inquiry and Exploration

When setting up learning centers, remember the following:

- Learning centers should give children the opportunity to make choices, problem solve, and create. If the activity chosen does not fulfill these expectations, rethink the activity. Giving children a pre-made page is not a good activity for a learning center. For example, a coloring book page does not help a child make choices, problem solve, or create.

- Each learning center should have a goal or purpose. Keep in mind the developmental guidelines for young children and create learning center activities that have a purpose.

- Organize learning center activities so that children can independently function at the center. (Make arrangements to help any child not capable of functioning independently).

- Learning center activities and materials should be open ended enough to encourage children to extend the activity or create an alternative activity.

- Adjust learning centers if children lose interest or the activity is not positively engaging for the group.

Learning Centers for Literacy Centers

The role of literacy centers is to offer engaging, hands-on learning activities that promote reading skills and an interest in reading.

Literacy centers are not meant to be a supplement to large-group, small-group and one-on-one literacy and reading lessons. Literacy centers take time to set up and organize; however, when they are done well, they can be a wonderful classroom management tool that offers rewarding learning opportunities for students. The following are suggestions for literacy centers:

- Literacy centers should be attractive and comfortable.
- Label literacy centers for a limited number of students, generally one, two, or three at a time.
- Set up literacy centers to be relatively independent learning opportunities. First introduce students to the activities, supplies, goals, and rules of each literacy center.
- Vary literacy centers to address a variety of learning styles and interests.
- Allow every student the opportunity to visit literacy centers. Using literacy centers as a reward for those students who have finished their work is appropriate as long as all students have an opportunity at some point to participate. In some cases, those who need the literacy center activities the most often have the least opportunities to visit them.
- Change or update literacy centers at least every few weeks to reduce boredom and present new learning opportunities.
- Involve students in creating decorations, labels, or rule lists for literacy centers.

Examples of Literacy Centers

Library Center. Most classrooms have a library. Transform the library into a literary center by combining a set of theme-related books with an inviting reading area. For example, use a plastic swimming pool with a few pillows and a picnic basket of books on sea animals.

Listening Center. A literacy listening center has books on tape or CD, along with headphones so that students can read along with the books. Another great option is to have a recorder that children can use to read and record themselves.

Game Center. A game center for two or three players can be an effective literacy center choice. Depending on grade level, games such as letter bingo, word bingo, Scrabble, or spelling dice can reinforce reading skills.

Name-this-Story Center. A name-this-story literacy center offers a variety of printed, age-appropriate stories that students are given the opportunity to title. Students can create a book cover with their chosen title as well as an illustration.

Keep in mind that the goal of well-planned literacy centers is to build reading skills and an interest in reading.

Learning Centers for Differentiated Instruction

Differentiated instruction is a philosophy of teaching that advocates the teacher adjusting and adapting instruction based upon the students' individual needs. Rather than forcing all students to move lockstep through a curriculum, the teacher identifies individual student's needs and learning preferences and provides a variety of learning experiences. Learning centers support differentiation.

Suggestions for Success with Learning Centers

- Start out with only two centers: one teacher-led activity and one independent activity. Add additional centers as students become more comfortable.

- To reduce persistent student questions, spell out very clear directions. Laminate and post these directions.

- Train student how to work the centers. Once students are introduced to the expectations and how the rotation among centers works, only a few students will need extra attention. Use resource teachers, aides, or parent volunteers to help manage these students through the centers.

- Be sure to have a visible timer to help students manage their time and movement through the centers.

- Use groups of three to five students at the centers. An odd number discourages pair conversations and encourages the group to work together.

- Have a diagram for students that actually shows the rotation schedule and locations of the centers around the classroom.

- Ensure that all materials are available at each center. It is often helpful to have all of these contained in one envelope or plastic bag. Have students return items to these containers after completing the activity.

- Have self-checking center activities; provide an answer key that students can use to check their own work.

- If you have access to one or two computers on a regular basis, set up several of the centers around technology application.

Learning Centers for Developing Independent, Engaged Learners

Learning centers get students up and moving and are an interesting way to introduce a new topic, text, or concept. Learning stations require a fair amount of preparation and monitoring to ensure a valid experience. They work best when a classroom can be sectioned into four or five smaller areas and students are given an activity sheet (guiding questions, thoughtful questions, or tasks) that must be answered or completed at each center. Each center should be geared toward a different aspect of the topic and challenge students. The centers can be visited in any order, can be visited by more than one student at a time, and should provide a comprehensive understanding once all centers are visited.

For example, if you are teaching *The Great Gatsby*, by F. Scott Fitzgerald, you could design the centers to give students a general understanding of the novel, the author, and the Roaring '20s in America. One center might have music for students to listen to jazz and write their thoughts. A reading location might provide a biography of Fitzgerald from which students record interesting facts. A poetry corner might challenge students to write their own beat poem, or an interactive video station might teach students the Charleston. Your role is to facilitate the activities, ensure that the students are on task, and answer clarifying questions. Learning centers put the weight of learning into the student's hands and provide a more authentic experience than traditional lecturing.

Learning centers can be designed to fit virtually any and every curriculum at all levels, especially language arts, social studies, science, foreign language, math, and fine arts. They are an excellent way to incorporate many skills and concepts as well as state learning standards. Centers can be used to supplement instruction or provide review for an upcoming test or end of chapter/unit assessment.

The following are examples of different learning center activities. Although these examples come from a language arts curriculum, they can be adapted to fit nearly any subject area.

Vocabulary Center. Students at this center develop skills in vocabulary by completing a vocabulary chart. The chart contains four columns labeled "vocabulary word and page number," "context clues," "my definition," and "actual definition." Using actual sentences from the book written on sentence strips, students identify the underlined vocabulary word and the page number where it can be found. Students then use context clues to discover the meaning of the word on their own.

Compare/Contrast Center. At this center students complete a thinking map, or graphic organizer, to compare and contrast two characters from the story. An example of a thinking map is a Venn diagram.

Journaling Center. You can use a journaling center in a variety of ways. Post a picture that goes along with a theme or character and have students reflect on what the picture depicts or how the character feels. Students can put themselves in the character's shoes or the overall story to write about their thoughts and feelings about what is occurring.

Reciprocal Teaching Center. Give students a reciprocal teaching task prior to them participating in the center activities. Tasks include summarizing, clarifying, predicting, and questioning. Students complete their tasks ahead of time so that once it is time to work at the center, they can come together and discuss their findings with group members. The group then makes a poster with four sections (one for each task), and writes down the information pertaining to each of their tasks.

Memory. This center is the ever-so-popular Memory game. Design the cards for Memory using the story in a variety of ways: vocabulary cards with definition cards; character cards with description cards; literary element cards with example cards. The cards can be made by the students or by you.

Visualization Center. This center allows students to represent their interpretations of the story. Students work individually or as a group to draw a scene or particular character from a book. Students should choose a scene that is memorable for them, include the sentence(s) they are visualizing, and cite the sentence(s) with page numbers.

Some center activities require whole-group work while others are meant to be completed independently. Still other centers offer students the choice to work together or alone. Since center activities require groups, you can form cooperative groups based on student ability or use differentiated instruction.

To apply this section to other curricular areas, break down the focus into workable pieces. For example, in a science class (specifically a lab), workstations may be broken down into hypothesis development, refinement, and conclusion; experiment development; procedure and data acquisition; and recording and analysis. In a social studies classroom, a teacher might break a history lesson into stations including primary source material, timeline development, cultural implications, geography and mapping, and connection to current events.

Learning Centers for Sequential Student-Centered Learning

Learning centers provide a more student-centered approach to instruction. When you facilitate learning to culminate in a performance task (typical in Quadrant D Gold Seal Lessons), often you have several activities and formative assessments that lead up to the task. Not every student proceeds at the same pace through those formative steps. Learning centers provide flexibility for students as they acquire the necessary skills to complete the performance.

Learning centers are also beneficial when you have limited resources in the classroom. For example, if you only have three or four computers and students must do an Internet search, set up a learning center where students in sequence groups use the computers for research. Likewise, if students in a science lab have to use a microscope and you have limited microscopes, you might use a learning center.

When setting up sequential learning centers, break down the unit of instruction and identify the major activities that students will engage in to get to the final performance. Assemble resources and materials for each of the centers, and create specific directions for students.

Decide if students will complete the centers individually or in small groups, and give students a full roadmap of each of the centers that must be completed. Students are usually required to master all of the learning center requirements, even though they may do so in differing order or in differing amounts of time. In this manner, learning centers ensure that every student reaches a level of proficiency. Frequently, learning centers have a formative assessment that is part of the overall unit.

Sequential learning centers can be a very engaging form of instruction. While they require more advance planning and conditioning of students to take responsibility for their own learning, they efficiently use limited resources and teach students to be independent learners.

Choosing Learning Centers

You have a variety of choices to present academic content. You have the choice not only to teach (or not to teach) with learning centers, but also to choose the sub-categories of content of each center, nature of activity, form of assessment, and time structure. Some teachers, especially in later grades, think that learning centers are not for them because of a potential loss of control. They cannot envision their students working responsibly without direct supervision and close monitoring. However, once teachers understand the practices of effective learning centers, many teachers choose to consider them.

References

Developmentally Appropriate Practices in the Early Childhood Classroom. NAEYC, 1995.

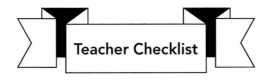

Teacher Checklist

Yes   No

☐   ☐   The learning centers have a clear purpose.

☐   ☐   The purposes of the learning centers are communicated to students.

☐   ☐   All materials necessary for the learning centers are prepared in advance.

☐   ☐   Students have clear directions to follow in each of the learning centers.

☐   ☐   Directions are written out for students to follow to reduce additional questions of teacher.

☐   ☐   Sufficient time is allocated for students to work in learning centers.

☐   ☐   Careful consideration is given to the assigning of groups for learning center activities.

☐   ☐   Learning center activities are varied and appeal to different learning styles.

☐   ☐   Students are encouraged to take responsibility for their own learning in using learning centers.

☐   ☐   The classroom facility provides adequate space for learning centers.

☐   ☐   Students are given the opportunity to reflect on experiences using learning centers.

K
N
O
W
L
E
D
G
E

APPLICATION

Logical and Independent Thinking

What Is Logical and Independent Thinking?

Logical and independent thinking is thinking deeply about an issue, taking a point of view, developing a logical argument, and defending a position. One of the goals of striving for rigor and relevance is to raise the level of student thinking. Several strategies in this handbook and the first volume include strategies that raise the level of student thinking. In *Effective Instructional Strategies, Volume 1*, the strategies of Socratic seminar, problem-based learning, project design, and research are all correlated with high rigor. In this handbook, summarization, compare and contrast, and technology-related strategies increase student rigor. Lessons that fall in Quadrants C and D of the Rigor/Relevance Framework require students to problem solve and be creative.

Logical and independent thinking is germane to rigor-related strategy; it requires analysis, synthesis, and evaluation. Logical and independent thinking differs from other strategies in that it uniquely requires students to seek independent ideas and develop a logical rationale for those ideas. In the realm of 21st-century learning, students need to be able to think differently, seek new solutions, and advocate for those solutions.

Logical and independent thinking can be best understood by looking at the three types of thinking that make up the strategy — critical thinking, creative thinking, and persuasive thinking. Logical and independent thinking is not a specific activity but more a broad-based approach to encourage higher level thinking in student work. Concentrate on these three thinking skills to build students' capacity to think independently and logically.

Critical thinking includes being analytical, differentiating fact from opinion, and identifying problems. Critical thinkers can analyze a situation. Creative thinkers identify innovative solutions that are not apparent to others. Finally, persuasive thinkers convince others to support their innovative idea. Persuasive thinkers draw us in to support their ideas.

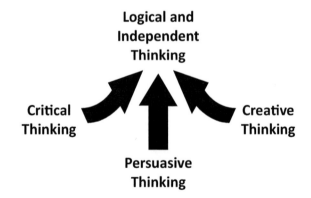

Defining Critical Thinking

There are several definitions of critical thinking. In essence, critical thinking means being analytical: examining the evidence and then making a reasonable judgment to evaluate a situation, a product, a presentation, or a piece of writing.

The key elements for student learning are as follows:

- Reserve judgment. Avoid jumping to conclusions and making false assumptions.

- Defer agreeing with any statement until confirming the credibility of the source or verifying with other sources.

- Keep an open mind and use keen observation to collect related evidence.

- Make judgments and evaluate based on observations, evidence, and analysis.

Activities to Develop Critical Thinking

Fact or Opinion

When viewing a commercial or listening to a presentation, people are often misled into thinking that opinions are facts. One of the first skills in moving toward logical and independent thinking is being able to distinguish fact from opinion. Knowing the difference is an important part of thinking critically. A fact is a statement that can be proven. It is generally about something that has happened in the past or is happening now. It is often based on the experiences of many people. Facts often involve numbers and specific measurements. On the other hand, an opinion is a statement that is generally a belief of an individual or a small group of people. Opinions are often made about things that could happen in the future.

Inference

Sometimes we can only make indefinite conclusions about statements that we read or scenes we observe. These conclusions are called inferences. An inference is a statement made about possible underlying causes. For example, a student is late for school. We might infer that the student overslept and missed the bus, or we might infer the student does not care very much about school. In both statements, we are making assumptions. Several possible conclusions could be true. Before converting an inference to a fact, collect evidence.

Challenge students to consider all of the possibilities for the underlying cause of something and then have them collect evidence to eliminate inferences not supported by the research. Help students avoid poor reasoning. This occurs when students jump to conclusions and assume that one of the opinion-based inferences is a fact.

Teacher Behaviors for Critical Thinking

- Require justification for ideas and probing for reasoning.
- Confront student with alternatives and thought-provoking questions.
- Ask open-ended questions.
- Hold students accountable for class discussion.
- Allow ambiguity.
- Give students conflicting information they must think through rather than clear-cut materials.
- Maintain high standards and expectations for all students.
- Encourage students to draw generalizations.

Defining Creative Thinking

Creative thinking is looking at problems or situations from a fresh perspective that suggests unique solutions. Creative thinking can be stimulated by a free-wheeling process, such as brainstorming, or by making unique connections with other knowledge. No individual has a lock on creativity. Encourage each student to unlock the creativity he or she possesses by taking an old idea and mixing it, moving it, or building it into a new idea. Traits such as humor, laughter, courage, and calm help individuals break out of structured thoughts and making new combinations by reorganizing these thoughts (Kirby and Goodpaster).

Activities to Develop Creative Thinking

Brainstorming

Brainstorming during the creative thinking process allows for many ideas to be generated. Brainstorming should have no boundaries, so the mind can move from one thought to the next, allowing for the creation of ideas. These creative ideas can be evaluated, picked apart, and restructured at a later time to help solve a problem. Use of graphic organizers can be useful aids in brainstorming. Both brainstorming and graphic organizers are discussed in *Instructional Strategies Teacher Handbook.*

Kipling Method

Rudyard Kipling's method for defining problems used five sets of questions to help trigger ideas and solve problems. These questions may help students through a sequence to clearly define a problem. Questions might include the following:

- What is the problem?
- Where is it happening?
- When is it happening?
- Why is it happening?
- How can we overcome this problem?
- Who do you need to get involved?
- When will you know you have solved the problem?

These questions work because they are short and direct and can be applied to many different problems. The key is getting students to pose several questions, rather than a single question.

Opposites

Another approach to stimulating a creative solution to a problem is taking the opposite point of view. Before coming up with a genuine problem statement and alternatives to solve it, brainstorm among the group on how to make the problem worse. By doing this, students may discover the source of the problem and better develop a solution.

Metaphors

A metaphor is a figure of speech in which a word or phrase literally denoting one kind of object or idea is used in place of another to suggest a likeness or analogy between them. Metaphors can help individuals examine a problem or issue from a different perspective by highlighting different relationships or characteristics. Engage students in brainstorming metaphors and explain how they can further define or give new perspective to a particular problem.

Walk students through an example of a metaphor to analyze a particular issue. Say: "For example, a teacher is a gardener of knowledge." Ask students to determine how teaching students is like tending to a garden. Students may note that plants grow slowly just like children do, that plants need care and protection just like children do, or that gardeners feel pride in the growth of their crop just as teachers feel pride in their students. Have groups of students tackle or develop other metaphors.

Teacher Behaviors for Creative Thinking

- Provide students extensive access to knowledge sources.
- Rewards innovators.
- Welcome new ideas and new ways of doing things.
- Keep information free flowing.
- Provide adequate time to deal with problems and arrive at solutions.
- Encourage experimentation.
- Elicit many solutions for one problem.
- Develop a sense of trust.
- Wait for and listen to students' descriptions of solutions.
- List all solution methods on the board to promote reflection.
- Push individual students to try alternative solution methods.
- Promote use of more efficient solution methods.

Defining Persuasive Thinking

A persuasive thinker uses logic to convince people to adopt an idea or join a cause. A person that is rational and logical gains the respect of others and has a more supportive audience. Logic is not the only part of the persuasion process; effective persuasion also has an emotional appeal. A successful persuader is aware of "root elements: values, needs, biases, and beliefs (Kirby and Goodpaster)." Root elements activate emotions and a good persuasive thinker tunes into the audience's emotions. A persuasive thinker should have a strong commitment to the position being advocated and convey the message in a rational style. Persuasive thinkers often use examples with inductive reasoning, statistics, analogies, and cause-and-effect relationships.

Persuasion is the act of getting a person or group of people to agree with your views and beliefs or take action based on your information on facts and truths. For example, getting people to drink less sugar-based soda because too much sugar is not healthy is an act of persuasion. On the other hand, attempting to have people drink less soda and fruit juices because they cause cancer is an act of manipulation, especially if the presenter is receiving some type of benefit for this fictional information.

Activities to Develop Persuasive Thinking

Persuasion Map

The persuasion map is a graphic organizer that enables students to map out their arguments for a persuasive essay or debate. Students begin by determining their goal or thesis. They then identify three reasons to support their argument and three facts or examples to validate each reason. Instead of having to work in a linear fashion, students use the graphic guides to develop their thinking.

Convince Me! Persuasive Writing

Persuasive writing is an important skill that can seem intimidating to younger students. This lesson encourages students to use skills and knowledge they may not realize they already have. A classroom game introduces students to the basic concepts of lobbying for something that is important to them (or that they want) and making persuasive arguments. Students then choose their own persuasive piece to analyze and learn some of the definitions associated with persuasive writing. Once students become aware of the techniques used in oral arguments, they apply them to independent persuasive writing activities and analyze the work of others to see if it contains effective persuasive techniques.

Teacher Behaviors for Persuasive Thinking

- Encourage elaboration of solutions.
- Encourage debate and dialogue.
- Encourage logical thinking.
- Use inductive reasoning.
- Expect rationale for opinions.
- Ask students to elaborate.
- Ask for evidence.

References

Kirby, R. and J. Goodpaster. *Thinking: An Interdisciplinary Approach to Critical and Creative thought*, (4th ed). New York: Pearson Prentice Hall, 2007

Teacher Checklist

Yes   No

☐   ☐   Students understand the three forms of thinking that combine to create logical and independent thinking.

☐   ☐   Students are encouraged to be critical thinkers.

☐   ☐   Students are stimulated to be creative thinkers.

☐   ☐   Students are challenged to be persuasive thinkers.

☐   ☐   Student opinions are listened to.

☐   ☐   Students are challenged to support their opinions.

☐   ☐   Students are given opportunities to collect evidence to support their solutions.

☐   ☐   Students develop analytical style of thinking to examine problems.

☐   ☐   Students use brainstorming tools to create alternative solutions.

☐   ☐   Students are taught to select alternatives objectively, based on criteria.

☐   ☐   Students are given the opportunity to work on real-world problems that are relevant to them.

Manipulatives and Models

What Are Manipulatives and Models?

Manipulatives and models are tangible objects students create or use to facilitate understanding. These objects engage students in hands-on learning and can be used in all subject areas and at all grade levels.

Manipulatives can be used when a new concept is introduced, practiced, or reviewed. They provide students with a hands-on, visual way to represent abstract ideas. They also can differentiate instruction for learners. Manipulatives might be simple, everyday items, such as toothpicks or bingo chips, or more sophisticated items, such as those purchased from teacher's stores or educational companies. Manipulatives that students or teachers create in the classroom can be very effective because the students feel ownership toward them, making the experience more relevant.

A growing number of teachers want to include technology while using manipulatives. These manipulatives are called virtual manipulatives. They include those found on educational software or educational sites on the Internet.

There are a variety of ways in which to incorporate the use of virtual manipulatives in the classroom; some of which will be explored in this chapter.

Models can also be used when a new concept is introduced, practiced, or reviewed. They are equally as beneficial as manipulatives but typically more static. For example, a model of the solar system cannot be manipulated because the currently accepted order of the planets is not interchangeable. Models are typically created with simple items, such as cardboard, construction paper, or aluminum foil, but can also be pre-fabricated models. The growing trend to use virtual models also will be explored in this chapter.

Why Are Manipulatives and Models Useful?

To understand why models and manipulatives are so effective, we look to one psychologist's research and learning theory — Jean Piaget.

A brief summary of Piaget's research states the following: Children master concepts by progressing through three levels of knowledge — concrete, pictorial, and abstract. In addition, Piaget theorized that children are active learners. Manipulatives and models are useful because they help facilitate understanding at the concrete level and serve as an avenue to engage students in an active manner as they move to the pictorial and then to the abstract.

More About the Three Levels of Knowledge

One important idea to consider is the notion of "moving" from one stage to the next. Are students "moving on" or "moving through?" Does moving from one stage to the other suggest that the movement is strictly forward and that it is inappropriate to go backward? If the stages are interpreted as isolated, then how can a teacher feel comfortable with revisiting a previous stage to remediate the learning? Perhaps one interpretation of movement and these three stages is that one stage supports or reinforces the next stage, and if a previous stage needs to be revisited, then that can be helpful to a student who is not quite ready for higher-level/abstract thinking.

Concrete	Pictorial	Abstract
• Commonly known as the most basic level of understanding: "What do I do?" • Teacher first models a concept or skill using concrete materials. • Students need opportunities to play and practice with manipulatives. • Teacher needs to encourage students to verbally justify their thinking.	• Also known as the "semi-concrete" level of understanding: "How can I show what to do?" • Students draw pictures that align with the manipulatives being used. • Students need opportunities to play and practice with drawing pictures. • Teacher needs to encourage students to verbally justify their thinking.	• Commonly known as the most sophisticated level of understanding: "Why do I do it?" • Students use symbols and higher-level thinking. • Students sort out most information "in their heads" and clearly explain their thinking. • Students can be re-taught at this level if they do not demonstrate a prior understanding by reverting to the concrete and pictorial levels.

Learning Styles

Manipulatives and models are useful because they also address different learning styles. For example, a synthesis of research indicates that, on average, about 30% of students are thought to be tactile learners — students who learn best by being involved with a lesson that employs fine motor skills. When teachers consistently use more traditional instructional strategies, such as lecturing and writing notes, they are addressing only the auditory learners (and on some level the visual learners). So what typically happens to those students who are primarily tactile and kinesthetic learners? They are unable to keep up, unwilling to keep up, or worst of all, bored. Using manipulatives and models is a hands-on way to re-energize your teaching and re-engage your learners. The following table shows a few examples of how manipulatives and models can actually benefit all four types of learners: auditory, kinesthetic, tactile, and visual.

Learning Style	Manipulatives and Models
Auditory Students who learn best by hearing and talking	Lessons can be designed to include small groups of pairs; students discuss concepts and ideas while using manipulatives and models.
Kinesthetic Students who learn best by being more physically active	Lessons can be designed to include learning centers or stations so that students need to walk from one place to the next; manipulatives or models are set up at each learning center or station.
Tactile Students who learn best by using fine motor skills	Lessons can be designed so that while a teacher is lecturing, he or she is also modeling a concept or idea.
Visual Students who learn best by seeing	Lessons can be designed to include visual representation of a concept or idea using a model; students can also be required to create a model or set of manipulatives as part of the lesson.

Manipulatives

General Strategies for Implementation

Students need to become comfortable with the practice of using manipulatives. Here are a few general strategies to consider.

1. Before implementing a lesson using manipulatives, talk with students about how manipulatives are helpful for learning a new concept or skill. Be sure that you choose developmentally appropriate manipulatives for your students.

2. Give students time to play with the manipulatives before they use them in a more intentional manner. They will be curious about them, so build in time for students to examine them individually, then in pairs or small groups.

3. Talk about the guidelines for using manipulatives. For example, they are not to be used as toys to be thrown around the classroom or at each other. They need to be gathered at the end of the lesson and properly put away for future use. Encourage students to be respectful of the materials used in the classroom by asking them where the manipulatives should be located for easy access. When you co-create a shared responsibility, students are more likely to feel empowered.

4. Build in a lot of time to demonstrate how the manipulatives will be used. Set the stage for the lesson by showing as many examples as possible.

5. Before allowing the students to proceed with the lesson, ask them to write down their observations about what you demonstrated. This will help you understand if the students have a good idea about how to use the manipulatives to develop conceptual understandings and procedural skills.

6. Have students record their observations after the lesson is over. This will help you determine if the manipulatives were developmentally appropriate and used appropriately or if the manipulatives were not helpful to the students.

Benefits of Using Manipulatives

- Students have control of how they are used.
- Students are provided with hands-on learning experiences.
- Manipulatives facilitate a deeper understanding of concepts by presenting problem-solving approaches in different ways.

- Students have more flexibility to explore and discover concepts and skills.

- Learning becomes more engaging, active, and student centered.

- Students can be creative and find other ways in which manipulatives might be used.

- All sensory learning styles can be addressed if lessons are designed with all four learning styles in mind.

- Cooperative learning opportunities facilitate development of social skills and working as part of a team.

- Students can co-create the manipulatives and feel more of a sense of ownership and responsibility for their own learning.

Challenges of Using Manipulatives

- Manipulatives might be used inappropriately or become lost or stolen.

- Students can easily become distracted from the purpose of their use (might be interpreted as toys rather than educational tools).

- Hand-made manipulatives can be poorly designed, resulting in the students becoming disgruntled by having to make them again.

- Pre-made manipulatives might not be available or too expensive.

Virtual Manipulatives

Virtual manipulatives are Internet-based representations of concepts and ideas. There has been much discussion among educators regarding the efficacy of virtual manipulatives in the classroom because some people do not consider them true manipulatives. If students cannot physically touch them, how can they be manipulatives? In general, virtual manipulatives are just another way to engage learners in discovering, reinforcing, or reviewing concepts and ideas. They are useful in conjunction with hands-on manipulatives.

Benefits of Using Virtual Manipulatives

- Most websites provide activities that provide timely feedback. In some cases, a student knows immediately whether an answer is correct or incorrect.
- Virtual manipulatives can be more explanatory than concrete manipulatives.
- Graphics can be more dynamic and engaging.
- Teachers with Internet access in the classroom can easily find sites to suit learning needs.
- The teacher saves time by having manipulatives instantly available (instead of having to make them or look through stores).

Challenges of Using Virtual Manipulatives

- Students miss the tactile experience by not being able to physically touch manipulatives.
- Some students are not comfortable or familiar enough with how to use a computer or how to navigate through a particular site.
- Not all content at all grade levels is available.
- Not all classrooms have sufficient technology.
- Technology might be too geared toward abstract thinking for students who need more practice at the concrete and/or pictorial level.

Models: General Strategies for Implementation

A model is typically a full- or small-scale representation of an object. Determine the best types of models to create by considering the following:

- rigor and relevance of the lesson
- skill levels of students in designing models
- cost and availability of materials
- time needed to complete the model
- use of the model in the current lesson and for future lessons

Students need to know why they will be creating a model within a particular lesson. Here are a few general strategies to consider.

1. Identify clearly the situation for which a model will be built. Provide students with a design brief that states the situation and an example of a model that can be built.

2. Have students brainstorm about the situation and write down all the information they can think of related to the situation.

3. Check in with students after their brainstorming session. Have a group discussion about details including the way the model will function and how it might look.

4. Begin the process simply and slowly. Building a model takes time, so keep the complexities out of the process until you see how the students are progressing.

5. Allot enough time for students to work on the model in the classroom, or offer guidance about how they can work on the model outside of the classroom.

6. Encourage students to document their thinking by keeping a record of both the creative and analytical steps in the process. Remind them that the focus is not solely on the end product but also what they are learning along the way.

7. Remind students that they don't need to "get it right" the first time. Part of the design process is taking risks and modifying what doesn't work or look the best.

8. Provide students with a rubric or scoring guide to help them achieve the best results. Clearly state the scoring criteria so that students can modify their models if certain goals are not specifically met.

Benefits of Building Models

- Students have control of how they are built.
- Students have a wide variety of choices, from selecting appropriate materials to use to how the model will be presented.
- Students are provided with hands-on learning experiences.

- Students have more flexibility to integrate concepts and skills.
- Learning becomes more engaging, active, and student-centered.
- Students can be creative. You might be surprised at how their thinking is translated into three dimensions.
- Cooperative learning opportunities facilitate development of social skills and working as part of a team.

Challenges of Building Models
- Students might not feel that they are creative enough to fully participate.
- Students can become discouraged if they need to keep modifying the model to meet the teacher's criteria.
- One or two students might be too involved in a group process, omitting the ideas and input of others.
- Materials might be unavailable or too expensive for what students really want to do.

Virtual Models

Similar to virtual manipulatives, these are also Internet-based representations of concepts and ideas.

Benefits of Using Virtual Models
- Usually free and available to the entire class (if the necessary technology is provided for the students)
- Can have more dynamic and engaging graphics
- Do not require time to design a plan
- Do not require time to build and modify
- Often come with specific directions about how to navigate the site to help students become more confident with working independently
- Keeps the classroom free from messes

Challenges of Using Virtual Models

- Students can be missing out on exploring their own creativity and problem-solving skills by not designing, planning, and making the physical model.

- Some students are not comfortable or familiar enough with how to use a computer or how to navigate through a particular site.

- Not all content at all grade levels is available.

- Not all classrooms have sufficient technology.

- Some students do not like being taught by a machine and would prefer more interaction with the teacher.

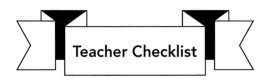

Teacher Checklist

Yes   No

☐   ☐   Students are informed about the reasons why manipulatives are being used.

☐   ☐   Developmentally appropriate manipulatives are selected.

☐   ☐   Students are provided time initially to play with the manipulatives and ask questions about them.

☐   ☐   Students are provided clear guidelines for how to use the manipulatives.

☐   ☐   Enough time is built into the lesson for me to demonstrate how the manipulatives are to be used.

☐   ☐   Students are provided with sufficient time to write down their observations about the demonstrations.

☐   ☐   Students effectively use manipulatives to develop conceptual understandings and procedural skills.

☐   ☐   Virtual manipulatives, if used, are in conjunction with concrete manipulatives in the lesson.

☐   ☐   Students search for virtual manipulatives on their own and report their findings.

☐   ☐   Students are provided with sites for virtual manipulatives that are pre-approved.

☐   ☐   Students in pairs or small groups treat each other with respect.

☐   ☐   Students have sufficient time to design an initial model and use a scoring guide or rubric to guide their work.

K
N
O
W
L
E
D
G
E

APPLICATION

Physical Movement

Why Do We Need Movement in the Classroom?

It is important to create a classroom environment that stimulates learning in all students. Physical movement is one of the most important instructional strategies a teacher can use in the classroom today. By using movement techniques to assist delivery of content material, a teacher can address all standards, connect across content areas, improve test scores, and have a profound effect on a student's life skills. Movement does not mean just getting up out of a desk and moving to another part of the room; it means incorporating short bursts of physical movement to increase oxygen intake, awaken the brain, and refocus student's thinking and experiences.

Obesity in our population today has grown at an alarming rate. The statistics now show that approximately 25 million kids are overweight or obese, and the lack of physical movement is the leading cause of this epidemic. With intense focus on high-stakes testing and extensive use of multimedia, our students today are the most sedentary generation that has ever existed.

American children have the highest obesity levels in the world. The present generation of children is predicted to be the first not to outlive parents. Not only is the lack of movement affecting the physical health of our children, but also it is affecting the emotional and intellectual health of our students. The Centers for Disease Control and Prevention found that movement and physical activities enhance learning in the classroom.

An important component that is directly related to the need to increase movement is one's inner ear. Movement stimulates the inner ear as well as the cerebellum. Sensory data is regulated in the inner ear and helps one to maintain balance, to turn thinking into actions, and to coordinate movements.

What We Have Learned from Brain Research

Brain research has shown that increased physical activity does improve cognition. When the brain is active and linked to physical activity, it produces a chemical that helps neurons communicate. The brain is better able to retain information, leading to improved understanding, comprehension, and information retrieval rate.

Exercise also positively affects the levels of neurotransmitters, such as glucose, which stimulate cognition. Creating more movement in the classroom helps students' bodies create more blood flow to brain cells, increasing overall blood circulation. By increasing the oxygen levels in the brain through simple physical activity, students can show marked increases in attention levels, short-term memory, processing speed, planning, sequencing, and self-monitoring.

Active instruction in the classroom can help to reduce students' stress levels. Stress stimulates the adrenal glands to produce a chemical called cortisol. When cortisol is present in high levels, the brain is less capable of planning, judging, and problem solving in alignment with the higher order thinking skills.

The brain is activated through the body's motor system. Movement in all forms plays a very important role in memory and mental cogitation. By embedding physical movement in your daily lessons, you can engage both the mind and the body, allowing the brain to function at its peak level.

Achieving 21st-century skills may be an ambitious goal to help our students become proficient in a global society; however, unless physical movement is a regular part of instruction, student thinking and achievement will likely decline.

How Can I Do This? My Plate Is Full! — How Can You Not?

The students in today's classroom are sedentary for the majority of the time they are in school despite what research is telling us. Daily stretching, walks, dancing, drama, seat-changing games, brain busts, and classroom energizers are simple techniques to integrate into the content areas and can be done with minimal preparation. The benefits of movement in the classroom can increase a student's academic and emotional performance in the following ways:

- improved emotional health
- improved self esteem
- increased alertness
- increased concentration
- improved mathematics, reading, and writing test scores
- less disruptive behavior
- higher rates of learning
- improved problem solving
- less school absenteeism

In Seattle, third-grade students who studied language arts concepts through dance activities boosted their reading scores by 13% in 6 months, according to Gilbert. Incorporating music and dance has increased math and verbal scores by using rhythm and repetitive beats and movements. In Canada, a study was conducted which increased vigorous aerobic exercises in the classroom. The results found a marked improvement in short-term memory, reaction time and creativity. When the movement activities are directly related to the academic theme and goals of the teacher, the students are more focused and better behaved.

Schools that have incorporated more physical movement into the classroom on a daily basis have seen positive effects on academic achievement, including increased concentration; improved mathematics, reading, and writing test scores; and reduced disruptive behavior. Even when time for physical activity reduces the time for academics, test scores go up. The students are engaged and healthy, and the teachers are having fun teaching.

Alicia Moag-Stahlberg, the executive director of Action for Healthy Kids, has been quoted as saying, "There absolutely is an association with grades and fitness levels. When schools had more kids in higher fitness levels, they had higher grades, math in particular." When you blend physical movement with learning experiences, comprehension and thought processing skills are greatly increased. After invigorating movement sessions, students are better able to focus on the next lesson and more receptive to information, improving cognitive skills.

With more physical movement in your classroom, don't forget to fuel the brain. The brain is composed of roughly 80% water and must be hydrated for optimal functioning. Have your students drink plenty of water throughout the day as dehydration can negatively affect their concentration. Upon entering school each year, students in Singapore are given a water bottle to carry with them each day. Teachers in Singapore have found that simply keeping their students hydrated keeps them alert and engaged.

The Time Has Come to Move!

When you incorporate a variety of movement activities into a classroom, an array of benefits emerges:

- sense of belonging
- improved self-esteem
- rest for the brain
- improved communication and listening skills
- opportunity for problem solving and higher level thinking
- environment that encourages laughter and fun while engaging learners

- improved motivation and discipline
- increased interest in attending and participating in class
- improved relationships

Struggling Students

Those students who are struggling readers or deficient in math skills have been shown to have fewer brain synapses, thus limiting the passageways of both hemispheres of the brain to communicate. This is often the result of a child's lack of physical movement, as movement stimulates an increase in body awareness, visual tracking, and coordination.

Students who struggle with reading often experience trouble with visual tracking, often due to the brain hemispheres not efficiently communicating. Utilizing cross-lateral movement to reinforce communication between the left and right sides of the brain has increased skills such as reading, writing, thinking clearly, and problem solving.

Movements that Support Learning

Physical movement seems to assist and improve the following:

- memory
- mental concentration
- planning and organizing
- test scores
- stress levels of students
- classroom behavior
- attendance
- attention in the classroom

Music

There is a strong link between academic achievement and steady beat competence particularly in math and reading achievement scores. Music stimulates right brain learning and makes the learning process more enjoyable. You can use music to introduce a new physical movement or activate vocabulary. By incorporating music and movement, students quickly make associations and connections to the material being taught. Rhythmic movement can be learned by moving parts of the body in enjoyable and interesting ways such as learning to dance.

Select appropriate music to align with the content you are trying to teach:

- Music should be used as an aid and not a distraction. Do not choose music with disharmonic patterns.
- If you want students to concentrate, select music that has regular periods with repeated phrases and patterns.
- A repetitive pattern of music helps with the repetitive nature of learning in math or grammar.
- Use music when asking the students to use their imagination to write descriptively.
- Walking and listening to music prior to lessons has been shown to increase verbal fluency scores in addition to making students feel better emotionally and mentally.

Movement Strategies

Cross-Crawl — This technique accesses both hemispheres of the brain simultaneously by moving opposite arms and legs together, either in a sitting or walking position. The arms and legs move in various directions to the beat of music or rhythm. Cross lateral movement stimulates the reconnecting of both brain hemispheres. This exercise is helpful for spelling, writing, listening, reading, and comprehension. Another option is to put the right hand across the body to the left knee as you raise it. Then put the left hand on the right knee just as if you were marching. Do this either sitting or standing for about two minutes.

Rocker — Sit on a chair and lift feet up. Rock one way and then reverse the direction. This releases tension in the lower back and sacrum. When the sacrum is free to move, the brain located at the other end of the central nervous system is activated as well.

The Calmer — This works well with students before a test to calm nerves and improve concentration.

- Stand or sit. Cross the right leg over the left at the ankles.
- Take your right wrist and cross it over your left wrist. Link up the fingers so that the right wrist is on top.
- Bend your elbows out and gently turn the fingers in toward the body until they rest on the sternum (breast bone) in the center of the chest. Stay in this position.
- Keep your ankles crossed and your wrists crossed. Breathe evenly in this position for a few minutes.

Where Am I? — During academic instruction, encourage students to stand and move around the room in groups or individually. This helps with knowledge of personal space and spatial awareness. A combination of the following activities will develop and improve vestibular systems and spatial awareness:

- spinning
- balancing
- jumping
- rolling
- turning

Those lacking in these concepts may have trouble in the following areas:

- reading
- organizing written work
- understanding abstract math concepts
- reproducing patterns and shapes

One-Minute Commercials — Have the students use drama to role play their learning or key points in a lesson.

Thinking on the Move — Have the students walk around the room, school, or outside while discussing a question(s) that you have aligned with your lesson. Moving while talking relaxes the brain to think on a higher level and relieves stress and barriers that potentially inhibit the student thought process.

Time Out for Yoga (or stretching of some form) — This allows students to get more oxygen into their systems, feeding their brain cells, bringing calm to the classroom, and decreasing stress.

Motor Activities — This can increase motivation and enjoyment of the learning process for spatial and kinesthetic learners. They gain benefits from doing and being engaged in the learning. Some examples include the following:

- Understanding a comma — Students walk while saying a sentence and pause to represent the purpose of a comma.
- Understanding number sequence — Students stand up and represent a number sequence using their bodies.
- Understanding a war — Students role play the war.
- Understanding an atom — Students become the atom.

Test Review — If you have the students move while reviewing cognitive information, retaining and recalling becomes easier.

- Students can walk in place while reviewing for a test.
- Use music or rhythm when working with math skills.

Jogging — Have your students jog in place when they are reviewing their spelling words or any other academic knowledge.

Game Time — Play hangman on the board when reviewing the states and capitals. Then have students do pushups or squats until they get the correct answer.

Up and Down — While the students are waiting in line or waiting for the bell to ring, have them do stretching exercises. Have students reach overhead and then touch their toes.

Cool Down — After doing a motor activity, try doing a cool down activity in order to get the students focused and ready to learn. Have students stretch and do deep breathing exercises.

Energizers — Simple physical tasks can give students renewed energy for engaging in more academic work.

- Have students toss a ball when doing review, vocabulary building, or storytelling.

- Human Knot — While in a circle, have students put their arms in and hold someone else's hand. Then try to unravel the knot without letting go of hands. This activity involves getting physically close to others, stretching, laughing, and problem solving.

- Group Juggle — Throw balls to others in a sequence, using each person's name.

Tips on Bringing Movement into the Classroom

- Short-term memory is best in the morning and least effective in the afternoon. Do activities that require quick recall early.

- Long-term memory is generally best in the afternoon. Lessons with repetition or emotional energy may be more meaningful later in the school day.

- Give students a mental break several times a day. When you find students becoming disruptive, staring off into space, or fidgeting, bring some movement into the classroom.

References

Centers for Disease Control and Prevention (CDC). *The Association Between School-Based Physical Activity, Including Physical Education, and Academic Performance.* Revised 2010

Gilbert, A. "Movement is the Key to Learning." Retrieved August 2010: www.newhorizons.org/strategies/arts/gilbert.htm

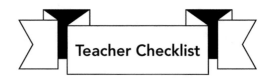

Yes   No

☐   ☐   Students have opportunities to develop their range of skills, talents, and interests through movement.

☐   ☐   A variety of physical activities are used to support and challenge students.

☐   ☐   Movement activities are used in a variety of settings.

☐   ☐   Movement includes both group and individual activities.

☐   ☐   Students are provided opportunities and time to engage curiosity and prompt inquiry through movement.

☐   ☐   Movement opportunities are provided throughout the day to all your students.

☐   ☐   Classroom space is organized to provide an active learning environment.

☐   ☐   Students are provided a rich and varied opportunity for play and experiences that stimulate students' creativity and imagination.

☐   ☐   The classroom is organized to allow students to consistently move around the space.

☐   ☐   The outdoor environment is a resource for movement and learning when planning a student's learning environment.

K
N
O
W
L
E
D
G
E

APPLICATION

Play

Play is not only our creative drive; it's a fundamental mode of learning.

—*David Elkind*

Play as a Learning Strategy

Play may not be the first thing that comes to mind when discussing instructional strategies. In fact, some may see play as a contrast to teaching: a teacher gives students time to play as a break from learning. However, play is a powerful learning strategy that develops important skills.

Play is related to several other strategies in this handbook — games, storytelling, artistic expression, physical movement, and manipulatives and models. Each of these strategies involves students completing open-ended tasks that enable them to use their imagination and creativity. In some situations play itself is a strategy that enhances student learning.

Even if adults do not initially understand the importance of play, children do. Many teachers and parents have observed the addictive nature of video games. These games are partly attractive because they invoke the natural play mechanisms in children. The human brain craves self-directed, open-ended, and joyful play.

In *A Whole New Mind*, Daniel Pink makes a logical argument for students to engage in more right brain learning — design, storytelling, empathy, symphony, play, and meaning — to make the transition from an informational age to a conceptual age.

Some educators regularly use play as a learning strategy. Many elementary teachers, particularly early childhood educators, recognize the value of play and build play time into the school day. However, educators beyond primary grades may be less comfortable planning this time due to the pressure for student academic achievement and higher test scores. When we remember that schools should be places of learning and not necessarily teaching, the appropriateness of play as a strategy becomes apparent. Educators should consider time to facilitate and encourage play.

Play is the most frequent way infants and young children learn. When children play with blocks, they learn three-dimensional reasoning that later becomes the foundation for geometry, physics, architecture, and engineering. When children sort blocks by shape, they practice fundamental math skills such as recognizing patterns and making comparisons. Working together with other children to create a playhouse lets children practice following directions, sequencing steps, and translating ideas into words and actions. Children learn a lesson on cause and effect by balancing blocks in a tower and then knocking them down.

Puzzles are another important tool used during play. Putting together puzzles helps children develop spatial reasoning, observe details, and practice hand-eye coordination. When children work together on a puzzle, they learn to take another's perspective, cooperate, and negotiate roles and material use. Puzzles can also be helpful for children to develop perseverance and cope with frustration.

The educator's role when using play as a learning strategy is to facilitate time to play. The teacher should encourage students to participate and socialize, as well as observe students being respectful and safe.

Challenging play builds stronger, more confident children. When instruction is all teacher centered, students are constantly looking to the teacher for affirmation of the "right" answer. In play there is no right answer; the experience is the intrinsic motivator, not an extrinsic comment from the teacher. Students judge what works and whether it is effective while reflecting on their own work and building confidence in what they do. Rarely do students engaged in play wait for someone else to judge that work.

Benefits of Play

- Play is an essential developmental activity for young children.
- It allows children to use their creativity while developing their imagination, dexterity, and physical, cognitive, and emotional strength.
- Play is important to healthy brain development. Through play, children at a very early age engage and interact with the world around them. Play allows children to practice adult roles, conquering their fears and developing the resiliency they will need to face future challenges.
- Undirected play allows children to learn how to work in groups, share, negotiate, resolve conflicts, and learn self-advocacy skills. When play is child driven, children practice decision-making skills, move at their own pace, discover their own areas of interest, and ultimately engage fully in the passions they wish to pursue.
- Research has shown that suppressing play in individuals results in poor human development, deviant behavior, and limited creativity (Brown). Further research in the engineering field has shown that engineers who have limited play experience are less creative when dealing with technical problems (Friedel and Liedtka, pages 30–37).
- Play is integral to the academic environment. It ensures that the school setting attends to the social and emotional development of children as well as to cognitive development. Play that allows peer interaction is an important component of social-emotional learning.

Increase Play in Schools

In this era of accountability, it seems we have pushed a standard curriculum down to kindergarten and pre-school in an effort to raise test scores.

Let's not "push down" the curriculum in an attempt to make a primary school with passive students in a teacher-centered classroom. Let's make the rest of school like pre-school: student centered and full of play opportunities. Let's allow children to discover patterns, culture, language and technology in a way that also teaches socialization, imagination, values, and joy.

As we apply brain research to teaching and learning, we must consider play. We were born to play. Play is how we learn and develop our minds and bodies; it is how we express ourselves.

Play leads to learning over time. Children seem to learn computer systems very quickly. One reason is that they are not afraid to experiment to see what works. They do not fear doing something wrong. If children get an undesirable result, they learn to do things differently next time. This type of problem solving is just one of many invaluable skills developed through play.

Types of Play

Play can take many forms and be categorized in several ways.

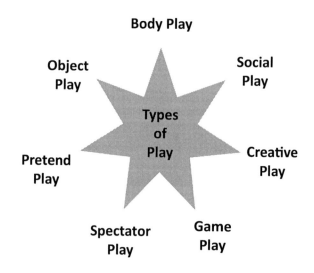

Body Play — Body play is simply any physical movement for release of tension, blood flow, and brain stimulation. Examples of body play in a school setting include the following:

- Reading while standing on one leg
- Bouncing on exercise balls and engaging in physical movement before working on a demanding cognitive task
- Climbing on equipment and structures on a playground

Object Play — Object play is the use of any manipulative. Object play not only builds fine motor skills and brain-hand coordination, it stimulates brain activity. Experimenting with hand-held objects has a direct influence on cognitive activity. The following are examples of object play in a school setting:

- Demonstrating a magic trick to make a point in a lesson
- Using a small object to pass or toss among students when engaging in group discussion
- Young students match shapes or place pegs in a pegboard

Social Play — Social play is driven by the urge to belong to part of a group. It can be creative free-form games among friends or "rough and tumble" play that involves physical challenges with others. Rough-house play often occurs within families and close groups of friends. It flirts with the fine line of violence, involves risk taking, and can result in injury to self and others; however, it also fulfills the development purpose of emotional regulation. Some may worry that this type of activity encourages children to become too aggressive, but within a monitored situation, rough-house play can actually help a child learn the self-regulation skills needed to know how and when this type of play is appropriate. Examples of social play in a school setting include the following:

- Playing physical games such as dodge ball and flag football
- Playing tag and other free-form games during recreation time

Pretend Play — The most common type of play for children involves nurturing their own imaginary people, places, and objects. This often occurs during role playing, one type of pretend play. During role playing children act out adult roles in specific creative scenarios. Pretend play enhances development of innovation and creativity, as well as builds other important skills. Deprivation studies have shown the importance of this pattern of play in order to develop trust for others and coping skills. The following are examples of pretend play in a school setting:

- Role playing a teacher, nurse, auto mechanic, firefighter
- Cooking a meal with imaginary food and utensils

Creative Play — Creative play is the process by which we germinate new ideas and shape and re-shape them. Creative play is similar to imaginative play in that the mind creates novel ideas; however, creative play fosters a frequent connection between imaginative ideas and the real world. A student constantly tries to imagine a new solution or design to a real world problem. Engineers, architects, and planners apply finely tuned creative play to design new buildings, products, and solutions. Examples of creative play in a school setting include the following:

- Creating a secret code for messages
- Building with blocks or other materials

Game Play — We use the term "play" games, and this is exactly what students do when they become engaged in structured games. This play might include timeless board games, such as chess or checkers, or classroom games to test memorized content. Games allow us to compete with others or to improve personal scores. Examples of game play in a school setting include the following:

- Participating in double-dutch rope jumping, hopscotch, or relay races
- Playing chess, Sudoku, board games, or word games

Spectator Play — Some games become a large part of the culture when many enjoy just watching others play. Spectator play is an observation of rituals and other performances that leads to enjoyment just as in other forms of play. While spectators do not gain the same degree of brain development as compared to other forms of play, spectators do derive benefits of satisfaction and attempt to imagine themselves participating at the same level. Examples of spectator play in a school setting include the following:

- Attending school sporting events
- Participating in pep rallies and cheerleading

References

Brown, S. *Play: How It Shapes the Brain, Opens the Imagination, and Invigorates the Soul.* New York: Penguin, 2009

Friedel, R. and J Liedtka, "Possibility Thinking: Lessons from Breakthrough Engineering," *Journal of Business Strategy* 28 (2007): 30–37

Pink, D. *A Whole New Mind.* New York: Penguin Books, 2005

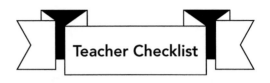

Teacher Checklist

Yes   No

☐   ☐   Students have opportunities to play periodically.

☐   ☐   Play in a school setting has a specific time, and students are informed in advance.

☐   ☐   Students are given choices and options in play activities.

☐   ☐   Time for play is sometimes spontaneous and not always during a rigid time frame.

☐   ☐   Students are adequately supervised to keep them safe in play activities.

☐   ☐   Students are provided multiple resources to play with during unstructured play time.

☐   ☐   Students are not graded on play activities.

☐   ☐   Students reflect on play experiences through conversation or writing.

☐   ☐   Students are given frequent breaks (15-20 minutes) for body play, such as physically stretching.

☐   ☐   Objects are used along with student discussion to stimulate brain activity.

☐   ☐   Students are given role playing opportunities to act out adult roles.

☐   ☐   Students are encouraged to be innovative in creative play activities.

KNOWLEDGE

APPLICATION

Service Learning

Service learning offers the opportunity for today's young people and tomorrow's leaders to learn, while addressing local needs.

—*Colin Powell, Former U.S. Secretary of State*

What Is Service Learning?

Service learning is an instructional strategy that actively engages students in meaningful service activities and promotes the acquisition of knowledge and skills. Service learning increases relevance by linking what students are learning in the classroom with opportunities to help others. It enables them to apply academic disciplines to practical, everyday problems. In the process, it provides a compelling answer to the adolescent's perennial question, "Why do I need to learn this stuff?" When students become immersed in community action programs and activities that contribute to the larger society, they cultivate leadership attributes and attitudes that follow them into adulthood.

In service learning students are encouraged to understand their service experiences in the context of the underlying societal issues being addressed. Students work with partners in carrying out their service activities, and the partnerships formed between schools and other organizations are collaborative, mutually beneficial, and meaningful. Service learning leads to successful outcomes in the community that are valued by those being served.

Service learning is not new. John Dewey conceived the idea in the early 20th century, but it did not take off until nearly 70 years later. Today, service learning programs are available in elementary and secondary schools, as well as in universities.

Although there are different perspectives on what constitutes service learning, quality practice for a program or activity meets several specific criteria. In essence, service learning requires learning objectives to be reached while performing some type of service work. It is different from other forms of experiential education in that both the recipient and the provider of the service benefit in some way and are changed by the experience. Service learning also requires participants to engage in reflection and critical thinking as they gain the specific values, skills, and knowledge required for success with their service work.

Service learning instructional approaches also gives students the opportunity to do the following:

- think deeply about complex community problems and alternative solutions
- identify and analyze different points of view to gain an understanding of multiple perspectives
- develop interpersonal skills in conflict resolution and group decision making
- actively seek to understand and value the diverse backgrounds and perspectives of those offering and receiving service
- learn how to transfer knowledge and skills from one setting to another
- recognize and overcome stereotypes
- have a strong voice in planning, implementing, and evaluating service learning experiences with guidance from adults

- participate in an environment that supports trust and open expression of ideas
- evaluate the quality and effectiveness of a community-based organization (www.servicelearning.org)

Service Learning vs. Community Service

Educators distinguish between service learning programs and community service, especially as they relate to the state standards of education. Generally, community service programs are enhancements or add-ons to classroom instruction. For instance, students in a U.S. government course might be expected to participate in 20 hours of community service during the semester or year. Activities could include attending city council and school board meetings, being involved in a political campaign, visiting senior citizen centers, and keeping track of their activities. Students gain a great deal of insight into the community while participating in community service, and they stretch their learning this way. Community service activities may be voluntary or mandatory and often are separately organized projects that do not include learning objectives, youth voice, student reflection, and formal assessments. Community service is also used as a form of punishment and sometimes has a negative connotation, especially for teens.

On the other hand, service learning programs tie into the course content more directly. Service learning is a way for students to become actively involved in specific community projects that instructors link to the curriculum to meet state standards of instruction. These projects are thoughtfully organized and orchestrated and hold students accountable for their community work. The projects include hands-on activities that relate directly to the course content and meet real community needs. For example, a science class might analyze water quality in a local stream and provide the results to a local pollution control agency, or a business class might offer income tax preparation services to local low income families.

Students involved in service learning, or community service learning as it is known in some states, make the connection between their service work and their course work. The activities are chosen because they meet clearly outlined objectives, so students are expected to participate in classroom discussions, write about their experiences, make presentations, and do other curriculum-related tasks. Part of a student's grade is based on the work relating to service learning.

Why Service Learning

Research reveals that service learning positively impacts students in the area of pro-social behaviors. It helps youth from diverse backgrounds learn to work together and accept one another. Through service learning, students acquire the following attributes ("Learning In Deed: The Power of Service Learning for American Schools"):

- increased personal and social responsibility
- greater self-awareness and self-esteem
- fewer behavioral problems and referrals for discipline
- more trusting and reliable attitudes and greater empathy
- increased civic responsibility and understanding of how government works
- higher grades on state tests of basic skills and improved grade-point averages
- improved motivation and initiative
- better school attendance rates
- gains in career awareness and positive workplace attitudes
- improvement in the overall school climate

A national study of the Learn and Serve America program of the Corporation for National and Community Service found that the effects of service learning are broad. It provides an opportunity for students to practice skills in real-life situations, promotes their caring for others, and extends their learning beyond the classroom. The community is strengthened because these programs enlist the efforts of parents, community leaders, and students to meet specific community needs.

Service learning varies greatly within different communities and schools. However, all service learning projects have similar characteristics that promote deep learning and involve critical thinking. These experiences are "positive, meaningful, and real" and address complex problems in complex settings ("Learning In Deed: The Power of Service Learning for American Schools").

Service learning works especially well when it incorporates the K-12 Standards for Quality Practice (www.nylc.org):

- **Meaningful Service** — The activities are meaningful and personally relevant.

- **Link To Curriculum** — It is an instructional strategy used intentionally to meet learning goals.

- **Reflection** — On-going and deep reflective activities challenge youth to consider their place in society.

- **Diversity** — Respect and understanding of diversity among all participants is promoted.

- **Youth Voice** — Young people have a strong voice in planning, implementing, and evaluating their service learning experiences with adult guidance.

- **Partnerships** — The collaborative, mutually beneficial partnerships address real community needs.

- **Progress Monitoring** — Participants continually assess progress toward defined goals and use the results to improve their work.

- **Duration and Intensity** — The activities last long enough and are intense enough to address needs and meet outcomes.

When aligned with these standards, service learning increases post-secondary matriculation and completion rates, helps students become self-sufficient, responsible citizens, and fully prepares students for the lives ahead of them. Students who participate in service learning experience positive outcomes in the following areas (Billing, 184–189):

- **Personal/Social Development** — Students increase self-efficacy, resiliency, multicultural awareness, and self-confidence. They are less likely to engage in risky behaviors that may prove detrimental to their futures.

- **Academic Achievement** — Students who take part in service learning activities have higher attendance, are more engaged, and make higher grades in school.

- **Citizenship** — Students become engaged in their communities, knowledgeable of civic and ethical responsibility, engaged in collaborative teamwork, and are more aware of the cultural contexts surrounding their communities.

- **Career Awareness** — Service learning experiences help students become more aware of career options and interests. They receive first hand lessons in the development of work-related behaviors, attitudes, and skills.

Planning for Service Learning

To start using service learning in the classroom, teachers should brainstorm with students about issues and problems in the community, state, nation, or world. Teachers can also have students do observational walks in their school or community to identify needs, conduct newspaper scans, meet with potential community partners, and design and implement community surveys. Questions to ask students during the planning phase are as follows:

- Is there genuine need?
- Who in the community would make good partners for this work?
- Does the community share the enthusiasm for the proposed activities?
- How will these activities fit into the existing curriculum?
- Is this work feasible based on the resources available?
- Can the school and community provide adequate supervision for students?
- Are the activities organized at a level appropriate for students' developmental levels?
- What can students learn from this work?

After considering these factors, teachers need to help students get the support of the school administrators and community partners. Each step of the process, as well as the roles of each participant, must be carefully outlined. Students should have a variety of participation options to choose from based on their interests and talents. It is important to keep in mind that the best programs for service learning are student centered and match the skills and talents of students with the needs of the community.

As students conduct their activities, regular time should be set aside for them to reflect on their work in ways that support a variety of learning styles. They should consider the impact of their work, how it affects others, and how their own behaviors and attitudes are changing over time. Teachers need to address the following questions when planning a service learning project:

- What course content lends itself to integration with a service learning project?
- How will content and skills be taught through service learning?
- What standards and benchmarks will service learning meet?
- What community needs will be addressed?
- Who will identify community needs?
- How will the work get done and who will be responsible for what?
- What issues must be addressed regarding permissions, supplies, transportation, and financial and personal needs?
- How will students make decisions about the project? Which decisions can only be made by teachers, and why?
- What prior skills, interests, and knowledge are needed for this project?
- How will students be prepared before starting the project?
- What reflection activities will be incorporated?
- What goals are to be accomplished, both for student achievement and for the identified need?
- How will student learning and progress toward goals be assessed?

Service learning provides multiple opportunities for integrated learning and interdisciplinary efforts, especially when it is approached school-wide or districtwide. Other important elements are broad support and commitment of the district and schools; matching the service learning role to the district and school missions; and professional development for teachers, parents, staff, and community participants.

Young people should be encouraged to have a strong voice in identifying community needs and planning activities in service learning. In addition, they should be actively engaged in evaluating the project and its impact. These processes give youth ownership and control over what they are learning. When schools empower students in this way, students develop leadership skills that help them become valuable members of the community.

The following steps will help ensure that students have ownership in their service learning activities:

1. Students should participate actively in investigating their community to learn about needs and resources.

2. Then, students should identify their personal interests and match them to local and national issues, as well as to needs in the community.

3. Next, teachers coach students as they research the issue on the Internet, read articles on the subject, conduct interviews with prospective partners, and gather data.

4. Students write an action plan that includes how they will develop personal leadership skills while working to alleviate a problem, increase public awareness on an issue, protect precious natural resources, organize others to take action, or other activities.

5. Together, students and the teacher find and contact the community or state organizations that match their interest area. Students with similar interests may form working groups.

Students keep records of their activities and participate in ongoing, guided self-reflection that becomes a major element of their experiences and helps them measure their personal growth in leadership (Pleasants, Stephens, and Pfeiffer 19).

Other Service Learning Project Ideas

The following ideas for community projects can tie into core curricula and other course content:

- Prevent alcohol or tobacco companies from placing billboards near schools.
- Help end child labor in developing countries.
- Prevent erosion and maintain water quality in surrounding areas.
- Prevent dumping of toxic waste into the storm drains of the city.
- Find after-school activities in safe neighborhoods for students.
- Set up tutoring and mentoring programs for under privileged children.
- Raise funds and build playgrounds for young children.
- Design and implement plans for a citywide animal shelter.
- Interview senior citizens and design an ongoing local oral history project.
- Research, restore, and maintain historic cemeteries.
- Work with the tourist center to design and produce a new guide to historic areas.
- Offer a computer technology class at the local library for community members.
- Develop brochures that outline the local health services available for low income families. Translate the brochures into other languages.
- Work with community leaders to plan and implement a career day for younger students.
- Provide a place and develop a program for senior citizens to exercise in the winter.
- Work with local scientists who study global warming by monitoring weather and posting findings on international websites.
- Work with local firefighting agencies and write a play for young children on fire safety.

Reflective Questions on the Service Learning Process

One of the requisite activities for quality service learning programs is student reflection on their experiences. As students engage in multiple forms of reflection, they think critically about their experiences and the issues they are addressing. Students can participate in small and large group discussions; make presentations about their service; compose letters of gratitude, encouragement, or recommendation; create skits or artwork; write music or poetry; and respond in any media about their service experiences. Ongoing reflection tracks their reactions and attitudes toward their service. Typically, teachers give students prompts for reflection during each stage of the service learning process:

Preparation Stage

- How do we determine a real community need?
- What constitutes a community?
- What is the root cause of an issue?
- What can our project reasonably address?
- What skills do we need in order to accomplish this project?
- What goals do we want to accomplish?
- How will we measure the impact of our efforts?
- How can we ensure a meaningful role for all participants in the project?
- What can we anticipate as a result of our service efforts?
- How can our project have a lasting effect?
- How can community organizations increase the impact of our activities?

Action Stage

- What steps are we undertaking?
- What do we need to accomplish these steps?
- Are we making progress on our plan?
- What adjustments, if any, do we need to make to the plan?

- What supports and resources do we need to complete our work?
- How well are we working with others? As a team?
- How do you feel about the tasks you're working on?
- Are our actions making a meaningful difference?
- How can we improve upon what we're doing?
- How are our actions affecting others?

Evaluation/Application Stage

- What was your best experience during the project, and why?
- What did you learn from this project?
- What did we accomplish?
- What challenges did we experience? Which ones did we overcome?
- How effective was the project in meeting our goals?
- How did our planning contribute to the effectiveness of our actions?
- What evidence do we have to document the impact of the project?
- What skills did we develop during the project?
- What character traits did we display or strengthen (responsibility, perseverance, courage, loyalty, etc.)?
- What could we have been done differently to enhance the effectiveness of our efforts?
- What other issues does the project raise?
- How can we apply what we've learned when planning our next actions?

Journals are one effective method of reflection because they offer metacognitive opportunities for students to think, deliberate, ponder, and reflect on their experiences and personal growth. Often, these journals are an eye into the deeper feelings that students are reluctant to share openly. Consider using social networking sites for students to write about their experiences as students are often comfortable using these sites. You can also ask adult community partners to join the conversations and reflections on the social networking site. Service learning nearly always uncovers fresh insights and profound sensitivities that students otherwise would not experience.

Resources

Schools interested in starting a service learning program will have no difficulty finding help from sources that explain each step in the process, whom to involve in the school and the community, ways to approach the community leaders, different models, and examples of successful projects that may be adaptable for use in other schools. The following are websites of some of the major service learning organizations.

- Learn and Serve America — www.learnandserve.org
- EarthForce (environmental service learning) — www.earthforce.org
- National Service Learning Partnership — www.service-learning-partnership.org
- National Service Learning Clearinghouse — www.servicelearning.org
- Service Learning Texas — www.servicelearningtexas.org
- Maryland Service Learning Resources — www.marylandpublicschools.org/MSDE/programs/servicelearning
- ServiceBook.org — www.servicebook.org
- National Youth Leadership Council — www.nylc.org
- KIDS Consortium — www.kidsconsortium.org
- What Kids Can Do — www.whatkidscando.org
- Youth Service America — www.ysa.org
- Youth as Resources — www.yar.org

References

Billing, S.H. "Support for K-12 Service Learning Practice: A Brief Review of the Research." *Educational Horizons*, 80(4), 184-189, 2002

Learning In Deed, W.K. Kellogg Foundation, *Learning In Deed: The Power of Service Learning for American Schools,* retrieved Aug. 2010: www.ecs.org/html/projectsPartners/clc/CLCLearningInDeed.htm

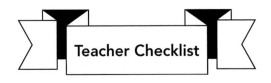

Teacher Checklist

Yes   No

☐   ☐   Service learning is connected to student learning standards.

☐   ☐   Service learning fulfills a community need.

☐   ☐   Students are given choices as part of planning service learning.

☐   ☐   Students take a lead role in planning services.

☐   ☐   Service learning engages all students.

☐   ☐   Service learning involves community partners.

☐   ☐   Students work in teams to complete service learning.

☐   ☐   Students write and reflect on service learning experiences.

☐   ☐   Service learning projects are planned well before engaging in the work.

☐   ☐   Students develop prerequisite skills and knowledge prior to engaging in service learning.

☐   ☐   Students are recognized for contributions to community as part of service learning.

☐   ☐   Students make recommendations for future improvement of projects.

☐   ☐   Service learning projects are evaluated by community partners.

☐   ☐   Service learning follows school procedures to ensure safety of students.

APPLICATION

Storytelling

Humans are not ideally set up to understand logic; they are ideally set up to understand stories.

—*Roger C. Shank*

Our Brains Remember Stories

Story is as old as language itself. Pre-historic civilizations told stories to share location of food and shelter and to warn of danger. They also shared exaggerated stories of the enormous and dangerous kill or the "one that got away." Stories are easier to remember than a grocery list, and one of the most effective mnemonic devices is to convert a technical list of items into a narrative story, thus making it easier to remember.

The popularity of movies and fiction literature show that we crave stories for entertainment or a diversion from life. Stories can also effectively convey meaning and concepts. Nursery rhymes and fables often describe in colorful forms important events or concepts. For example, the story of the tortoise and the hare is a vivid and imaginative way to convey the concept that perseverance is often more important than speed.

In many ways we are rediscovering storytelling as a communication tool. In our effort to refine teaching language skills, curriculum experts have often focused on memorizing the discrete tools of language: vocabulary, spelling, sentence structure, and literary technique. However, this is like giving a construction worker a set of tools and saying that he or she is a master builder. Effective language use takes practice as well as the proper tools. Just as students might practice writing a research report or business letter, a story can be a way to combine language into effective communication. Furthermore, storytelling can be used as a strategy in other subjects such as science and social studies.

What Is Storytelling?

Storytelling involves imagination and the use of language and gestures to create scenes in the mind of the listener. The more you know about storytelling, the better you can teach and model it for students. Stories are not fixed scripts that are always recited or read the same way; the good storyteller finds a new adjective or gesture to more deeply engage the listener each time he or she tells the story. Storytellers are often just as important as the story. While a joke may be exceedingly funny when told by one person, the same joke may fall flat when told by another. The delivery of the joke triggers our laughter. Effective storytelling intimately combines the storyteller and the story. A storyteller's cultural background and unique personal attitudes and experiences should come through in words and gestures. The unique character and voice of each teller brings to life a good story.

Benefits of Storytelling

Story exercises imagination, an essential for higher-level thinking. A quality education requires that we not only give children the ability to spell words correctly and create grammatically correct sentences but also encourage them to develop rich experiences with words and gestures through story. When we listen to a story, we do more than listen to the words and ideas: we connect with our emotions. Storytelling uses the logical brain's functions (language, a story line, sequences of cause and effect) to speak the conceptual brain's language of symbolic, intuitive, imaginative truths. Thus, storytelling stimulates the brain as a whole, promoting health and development.

Strategy and Student Work

Story can be both a teaching strategy and a form of student work. Since story is more engaging than straight lecture, teachers can use a story with narrative hooks and vivid images to introduce content and help students understand concepts. Teachers can also ask students to present the results of reading or research in the form of story. While it takes additional time to demonstrate for students the form of creating and delivering stories, students will be more engaged in learning and develop a form of communication that is a lifelong skill.

Effective Storytelling Skills

The following list details the characteristics of effective story telling. When students tell a story, these observable criteria may be used to evaluate the performance.

Voice

- Speaks with an appropriate volume for the audience to hear
- Enunciates clearly
- Avoids monotone
- Uses changes in vocal expression to clarify the meaning of the text

Gestures

- Expressively uses non-verbal communication to clarify the meaning of the text
- Avoids any body language that distracts from the storytelling

Focus

- Makes eye contact with audience
- Maintains a charismatic presence in space (stage presence)
- Stays in character of the story teller throughout the story
- Uses voice different from character voices if dialogue is used

Words
- Uses descriptive and articulate language
- Gives context to new words to help audience understand meaning

Setting
- Appears comfortable, relaxed, and eager to tell the story

Pacing
- Presents story efficiently and keeps listeners' interest throughout the story

Story Structure
- Presents clear and engaging opening
- Presents sequence of events easy for the listener to follow
- Tells story completely and presents clear ending

Innovation
- Employs unique or creative use of language, sound, or body language
- Creatively presents the sequence of events
- Artfully expresses or suggests perception of the meaning of the story through telling

Tips for Teacher Stories

- Tell or enact a story to illustrate the points made in Effective Storytelling Skills. Begin with personal tales before moving on to short stories, such as Aesop's fables. Select stories that are easily learned.
- Storytelling will require you to be loose, expressive, and even goofy at times. Some students may love storytelling, and some may hate it. However, because the ability to speak with comfort

and conviction in front of people is important to success in this world, stress the importance of storytelling so students are encouraged to improve their own skills.

- Prepare for your performance: write, practice, and rearrange the story; make notes to yourself; and view your performance on videotape or in the mirror. Then stand in front of your class, take a deep breath, smile, and just start talking. Trust yourself to know where you are going with the story and give yourself permission to change the timing, rhythm, sounds, facial expressions, and even a few words if necessary.

- Although you may hope to entertain your students, your purpose is to build literacy skills through storytelling. To keep the emphasis on language, help your students analyze the story. Ask students to summarize your story in one sentence.

Working with Students as Beginner Storytellers

Students initially may have a fear of telling a story in front of an audience. Impress upon them that the audience is essential; without an audience, there is no purpose to tell the story. Also, remind students that storytellers improve over time. No one delivers a perfect story the first time. When coaching students about improving their storytelling skills, always start with compliments about things they have done well. Help students develop, improve, and evaluate their performance using the following suggestions:

- Draw on a variety of sources when constructing your stories. Personal tales, or stories of real experiences, are a good first step since the facts are well known to you.

- Brainstorm. First write down some story ideas without considering how good they are. Now put one idea or memory into a sentence. Decide if you want to tell a story in the first or third person and what impact that will have on the story.

- Write down the sequence of facts. From there, add the details, descriptions, situations, time reference, and colors. Finally, layer the feelings and emotions. Choose your words carefully.

- If appropriate, put in a few sound effects, vocalizations, facial expressions, and silences. As funny as you may feel about talking out loud while you are writing, certain words sound better than others when they are spoken. Speaking out loud may help you with sentence structure and word choice.

- Practice telling the story to one person at a time. Keep changing partners. As your confidence builds, tell the story to small groups. When the story is well rehearsed, tell it to the class.

- Visualize the scenes: Who are the people in each scene? What do they look like? How do they talk, move, and stand? Imagine the action in the story. Use your imagination to add to the story.

- Use movement when telling the story. Audiences respond to physical movement, and it enlivens the tales. Moving also may put you at ease and help you convey ideas. Dull storytelling is often static and word based.

- Embellish adjectives. Practice selecting additional adjectives to describe a scene. [Note: Show students an image and ask them to come up with as many adjectives to describe the scene without repeating previously mentioned adjectives.]

- Practice using your eyes to hook the audience into the story. Storytellers talk directly to the audience. Using eye contact helps the audience feel your energy.

- Try to use three to five senses in your stories. Describe how things look and feel, including colors, scents, textures, and tastes.

- Watch the audience and learn from their reactions. When does the story cause the audience to lose interest? What words and gestures create interest? Adjust stories to engage the audience.

If you have students who have difficulty telling a story, meet with them individually. Encourage them to think about events in their lives, people, places, and celebrations. Let them know that we are all storytellers and that their experiences are worth sharing. Explain how you resolved difficulties in creating your story and assure them that they can do the same.

Making a chart or outline may help some students focus on different story elements. Others may get frustrated with concentrating only on specific parts of their stories and will need to deal with all the story elements at once. Encourage students to try alternative words and phrases out loud before committing to a final version.

Storytelling Ideas

- **A picture is worth 1000 words** — Choose a picture, such as a classical painting or a photograph with interesting people or characters, and have students create a personal story about the images in the picture.

- **Proverbs** — Have students use familiar proverbs to develop a story that illustrates a particular proverb. Proverbs might include the following:

  ○ The pot calling the kettle black.

  ○ A watched pot never boils.

  ○ You cannot have your cake and eat it too.

  ○ Haste makes waste.

  ○ It takes a village to raise a child.

  ○ A bird in the hand is worth two in the bush.

  ○ A stitch in time saves nine.

- **Animal stories** — Assign students an animal character and challenge them to create a story about a person they know who has similarities with the animal. Do not have students identify the person as this might be embarrassing; however, encourage students to illustrate a person using the characteristics of the animal.

- **Puzzle folktales** — Take a printed copy of a folktale and cut it into separate pieces by paragraphs. Give each student a different section or puzzle piece. Have students try to sequence the fable by putting the pieces together. Once they have assembled a sequence, have the students tell their story. As another option, give different groups of students the same story and see if the sequence and story is the same or different.

- **Story circle** — Have students sit in a circle. One person begins a story and stops after two sentences. The next person in the circle continues the story by adding two additional sentences until everyone has had a chance to contribute.

- **Local interviews** — Have students interview older people in the community to identify historic local, national, or global events. Students might obtain photographs from historical periods to illustrate their stories as they retell what they learned from older people. As a variation, students might role play characters in that particular historical period.

- **Family stories** — Have students tell stories of their family history. This might include descriptions of the number of family members and where they currently live or historical reference as to when their family came to this country. Students might interview family members to prepare for a story of family history.

- **Storytelling for younger students** — After students have practiced their storytelling skills, they might perform their stories for younger students or other classes.

- **1001 Nights Festival** — The legend of Scheherazade, the great storyteller, is that she told stories to a sultan for 1001 nights. Following this example, divide a story into short segments and tell stories over a period of time, peaking students' interest to return to the story in subsequent sessions.

- **Group story creation** — This is an activity that can engage several classes working together. Use a picture or painting as a trigger to stimulate a story. This same image is shared with several classes. For example, all fifth grade classes in the school might work collaboratively. The first class writes one paragraph to begin the story. The paragraph is then passed to another class that brainstorms and creates a second paragraph of the story. This two-paragraph story is then passed to another classroom, and the cycle continues until the story is completed. The classes might come together and listen to their collaboratively developed story.

- **Story from music** — Have students search and analyze musical lyrics to find a story. Challenge them to expand upon the story illustrated in the musical lyrics. In a presentation, students tell their story as well as play the music. This makes an excellent group project.

- **Broadcasting stories** — Once students create excellent stories, they might be broadcasted as presentations across the entire school community.

- **Multiple adjectives** — This exercise helps students practice using descriptive adjectives for storytelling. Have students sit in a circle and pass an object, such as a stone or ball, around the circle. Have a student identify one adjective to describe the object before passing the object to another student. The next student must identify a different adjective before passing the object around the circle.

- **Story of invention** — Take simple objects from the classroom, such as a pencil, paper clip, shoe, or piece of paper. Challenge students to create a story about how that object was invented and created for the first time.

Digital Storytelling

With the introduction of low cost, easy-to-use technology tools, teachers and students can enhance their stories with recorded audio and video. This has emerged into a separate strand of strategies known as digital storytelling. The Center for Digital Storytelling (CDS) is an international non-profit training, project development, and research organization dedicated to assisting people in using digital media to tell meaningful stories from their lives. Their focus is on building partnerships with community, educational, and business institutions. Using methods and principles adapted from digital storytelling workshops, the organization hopes to develop large scale initiatives in health, social services, education, historic and cultural preservation, community development, human rights, and environmental justice arenas.

The Center for Digital Storytelling (www.storycenter.org) offers Seven Elements of Digital Storytelling:

- Point of View
- A Dramatic Question
- Emotional Content
- The Gift of Your Voice
- The Power of the Soundtrack
- Economy
- Pacing

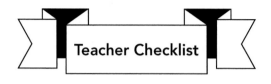

Teacher Checklist

Yes   No

☐   ☐   Your stories are related to learning objectives.

☐   ☐   Your stories have a specific learning intent.

☐   ☐   Your stories use expressive language and gestures.

☐   ☐   Your stories have a clear beginning and end.

☐   ☐   Your stories are kept to an appropriate length.

☐   ☐   Students are asked to analyze and reflect on your stories.

Student Stories

☐   ☐   Students understand the difference between story and memorization.

☐   ☐   Students use expressive language, gestures, and exaggerated voice for characters.

☐   ☐   Students speak loud enough for others students to hear.

☐   ☐   Students maintain a proper pace in telling the story — not too fast or too slow.

☐   ☐   Students maintain eye contact with the audience.

☐   ☐   Students' stories have a clear beginning and end.

☐   ☐   Students' stories keep attention of peers.

☐   ☐   Students' stories are appropriate in length.

APPLICATION

Summarizing

What Is Summarizing?

Summarizing is restating the essence of text or an experience in a concise form that retains meaning and important information. Summarizing and note taking require the ability to synthesize information by putting it into a new format. To summarize, a student must analyze information and organize it in a way that captures the main ideas and supporting details as well as restates it in the student's own words. Summarization is high-level, rigorous thinking because it requires analysis and synthesis, and research shows that it is among the most effective teaching strategies increasing student achievement (Marzano).

Fiction and nonfiction texts, media, conversations, meetings, and events can all be summarized. Students initially want to retell everything they have read, seen, or heard. However, summarizing is more than retelling; it involves analyzing information, distinguishing important from unimportant elements, and translating large chunks of information into a few short cohesive sentences.

Why Is Summarizing Important?

- Summarizing allows both students and teachers to monitor comprehension of material.
- Summarizing helps students understand the organizational structure of lessons or texts.
- Summarizing is a skill at which most adults must be proficient to be successful.

Summarizing integrates and reinforces learning of major points. This not only facilitates recall of the information but also allows the student to see connections and patterns in information. Ultimately this helps students use the knowledge when called for in other applications.

Students can summarize information in different ways including deleting information not important to the overall meaning of the text, substituting some information, and keeping some information. As students practice these strategies, they enhance their ability to understand specific content for learning.

Teaching Summarizing to Students

Before instructing students on specific strategies or procedures, consider the following items suggested by Rick Wormeli for summarizing success.

Activate Student's Background Knowledge — Students bring their own prior experiences and knowledge with them for every reading activity. Students' own viewpoints and thoughts on particular topics can lead to a variety of interpretations of the text or experience. Ensure that students have enough background information about the topic and activate that knowledge so a breakdown in understanding does not occur. You might have a class discussion or watch a related video clip to activate background knowledge.

Prime the Student's Brain (Setting Purpose) — Along with activating students' prior knowledge, offer students a specific reason or goal for reading a piece of text. Students who are given a purpose for reading are much more likely to retain information than those who are not. Also help students prepare for reading by advising them how to create their own purpose.

Identify Text Structure — Authors structure text based on content and topic. Students' familiarity with different structures can lead to a better understanding of how the material is presented and of the material itself. Some well-known text structures include enumeration, chronological order, compare and contrast, cause and effect, and problem and solution.

Following Clues — Help students become conscious of text by instructing them about the kinds of clues they should be looking for within the text. This may help with comprehension as well as summarization of the text. For example, detecting and noting the topic sentence can be extremely useful for determining the main idea of the piece. While sometimes located at the beginning of the paragraph, the topic sentence can also be in the middle or simply implied through fragments of text. The first and last sentences can also contain clues to the main points of the text. Coach students as they practice analyzing a text for topic sentences.

Offer Tools — Helping students become conscious and engaged about what they are reading is an important aspect of reading for meaning and summarization. "Good readers read text passages at least twice: once to get the general overview and then again to determine what is salient." Provide students practice and time to reread text to help them better understand the purpose for the reading.

Strategies such as making notations and marking the text help students record their thoughts while they read. These notes can help students gain insight into what is really important in the text and how they feel about it.

The following are several summarization tools and approaches.

Follow the Rules

One strategy for teaching students to summarize is to give them a consistent set of rules to follow. The following generic rules may be used for summarizing:

1. *Skip* unnecessary material.
2. *Delete* redundant material.
3. *Substitute* an overall term for lists.
4. *Select* a single topic sentence to begin the summary.

These rules closely follow the thinking process in summarization: *skip* and *delete* the less important information, *substitute* to shorten information, and *select* most important information. Students need to practice using these rules with close supervision to gain proficiency and develop study habits. When introducing summarization and these rules, create a game to see who can use the least number of words and still retain meaning. Use student peers as judges to evaluate whether or not a summary captures the meaning of the original text.

Retelling to a Specific Audience

Summarization may feel like busy work to students since they are usually summarizing information for you that you already know. Develop more authentic assignments in which students summarize information for a specific audience: a student who has not read the material, a younger student, or another adult with a specific interest. The student will practice summarizing information as well as making connections with the needs and interest of the audience. This real-world application of summarization may be much more motivating and helpful for students.

The following are rules for summarizing for an audience:

- **Make a connection** — Why is this material important to this audience?
- **Summary** — What is a brief description of the information and the most important aspects?
- **What next** — What are some specific suggestions for next steps? To locate further information? Learn more? Take some action?

Work with the Summary Frame

Summary frames are specific applications to give to students to use in specific summarizing activities. The following are types of frames that could be used in various teaching situations (Marzano). It is often useful to create a template or form for students to use with the appropriate frame.

- Narrative Frame
- Definition Frame
- Argument Frame
- Problem/Solution Frame
- Conversation Frame

Narrative Frame — The narrative or story frame is common when summarizing fictional writing and contains the following elements:

- Characters — Who are the main characters and what distinguishes them from others?
- Setting — When and where does the story take place? What are the circumstances?
- Initiating event — What prompts the action in the story?
- Internal response — How do the characters express their feelings?
- Goal — What do the main characters decide to do? Do they set a goal and if so, what is it?
- Consequence — How do the main characters try to accomplish their goal?
- Resolution — What are the consequences?

Definition Frame — The purpose of the definition frame is to describe a particular concept and identify related concepts. Definition frame should contain the following elements:

- Term — What is being defined?
- Set — To which general category does this item belong?
- Characteristics — What characteristics separate this term from other things in a similar category?
- Examples — What are some of the different examples of the item being defined?

Argument Frame — The argument frame contains information designed to support a point of view such as analyzing a historical event or current issue. It contains the following elements:

- Evidence — What information is presented that leads to the point of view?
- Claim — What statement or point of view is the focus of the information?
- Support — What examples or explanations are presented to support this point of view?
- Qualifier — What special circumstances or concessions are made about the point of view?

Problem/Solution Frame — Problem/solution frames introduce a problem and then identify one or more solutions to the problem.

- Problem — What is the problem?
- Potential solutions — What are the possible solutions?
- Best solution — What is the solution for best solving the problem?

Conversation Frame — A conversation is a verbal exchange between two or more people. Commonly, a conversation has the following components:

- Greeting — How do the members of the conversation greet each other?
- Inquiry — What question or topic was expressed or referred to in the conversation?
- Discussion — How did the discussion progress? Did either person state facts? Did either person make a request of the other? Did either person demand a specific action? Did either person describe specific consequences if the demand was not met? Did either person compliment the other?
- Conclusion — How did the conversation end? Was there any agreed upon follow-up action?

Teacher-Prepared Notes

Teacher-prepared notes are one of the most straightforward uses of note taking as a summary. They provide students with a very clear picture of what you consider important as well as a model of how notes might be taken. After the discussion of a piece of text, you might provide students a written or electronic copy of your notes. While you might think that handing out your notes only eliminates work for your students, the final objective is student learning. In some instances giving students a well prepared set of notes is more effective than having students struggle with a poor set of self-written notes. In addition, students can use your notes to evaluate their own set of notes.

Exit Ticket

An exit ticket is an ideal strategy when you only have a few minutes at the end of class to informally assess student learning. Students summarize a concept or idea related to the class, and this serves as their ticket to leave the class. Generally students write their summary on a small card or slip of paper and hand them either to you or a designated student upon departing class. You can quickly read these exit tickets to gauge a level of student understanding. If time allows, students might read their exit tickets to the class. The following are examples of typical exit ticket questions:

- Name one important thing you've learned today in class.
- Write/ask one question about today's content that has left you puzzled.
- Read this problem and tell me what you need to do first to solve the problem.
- Give me one example of how you would apply what you have learned today.

A good practice is to inform students in advance that there will be an exit ticket and provide them with a general description of what the exit ticket will be. This helps to prepare them for this activity and will lead to better responses.

Best Test

In this strategy, students are paired and grouped at the end of a unit to write what they consider to be the best test for that unit. Provide guidelines as to how many of each type of question to include. Students who create the test also write answers for every item. The student(s) whose test is selected receives an automatic "A" grade for the test and does not have to take it.

One-Word Summaries

Summarizing a topic into just one word can be a challenging task for students. They tend to think that more is better. When students are asked to develop a one-word summary, they must apply their critical thinking skills to investigate, read about, and analyze the topic. They must isolate the critical characteristics and come up with one good word that best fits the topic. After students have chosen their word, they must defend their word choice with a valid reason. What makes this a powerful strategy is not the choice of the one word but the development of the rationale. This strategy can be used as a classroom assessment for learning as students evaluate their own justification for word choice.

Think-Pair-Share

Think-Pair-Share is a summarization strategy that can be used in any content area before, during, and after a lesson (Lyman). The activity involves three basic steps. During the "think" stage, students ponder a question or problem. This allows for wait time and helps students control the urge to impulsively shout out the first answer that comes to mind. Next, individuals are paired up to discuss their answer or solution. During this step students may wish to revise or alter their original ideas. Finally, students are called upon to share their ideas with the rest of the class.

Put a visual on the board or screen to remind students of the steps.

Think-Pair-Share

1. **Think** about your answer individually.
2. **Pair** with a partner and discuss your answers.

3. **Share** your answer (or your partner's answer) when called upon. A variation is to have students write during the first step.

Write-Pair-Share

1. **Write** your answer individually.
2. **Pair** with a partner and discuss your answers.
3. **Share** your answer (or your partner's answer) when called upon.

Another variation is Think-Pair-Square-Share. In this strategy, partners discuss answers with another pair before sharing with the class. This activity ensures that all students are interacting with the information. You can use this activity as a formative assessment as you walk about the room listening to student conversations.

References

Lyman, F. "The responsive classroom discussion: The inclusion of all students" In: A. Anderson (ed.), *Mainstreaming Digest* (pp. 109–113). College Park: University of Maryland Press, 1981.

Marzano, R. et. al. *Classroom Instruction That Works*. Alexandria, VA: ASCD, 2001.

Wormeli, R. *Summarization in Any Subject: 50 Techniques to Improve Student Learning*. Alexandria, VA: ASCD, 2005.

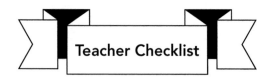

Teacher Checklist

Yes	No	
☐	☐	Students are given notice of expectations for summarization prior to introducing the information.
☐	☐	Students understand the difference between summary and memorization.
☐	☐	Students give consideration to the audience.
☐	☐	Students are encouraged to avoid rote recall of information in summaries.
☐	☐	Students are given a structure/frame for summarization.
☐	☐	All students practice summarization.
☐	☐	Students are encouraged to improve summarization over time.
☐	☐	Students are expected to defend their summary.
☐	☐	Students are encouraged to use their own words in their summary.
☐	☐	Students practice both written and oral summaries.
☐	☐	Students are given positive feedback on effective summaries.
☐	☐	Students are given encouraging and constructive feedback to improve weak summaries.
☐	☐	Forms and graphic organizers are used to guide and record student summaries.

Teaching Others

What Is Teaching Others?

An ancient Chinese proverb says, "Tell me and I forget . . . show me and I remember . . . involve me and I understand." As you move your students to Quadrant D thinking, provide them with opportunities to think in complex ways and apply the knowledge and skills they have acquired. Teaching others allows students to deepen and apply knowledge. The process involves students learning from and with each other by sharing prior knowledge, ideas, and experiences. While peer teaching usually takes place within the classroom during the school day, teaching younger students may take place outside of your classroom or even outside of the school day. In general, teaching others is a way to move from teacher-centered instruction to student-centered instruction so that students feel more comfortable with their own learning. This strategy can be used at all grade levels in all subject areas.

Why Use Teaching Others?

A recent conversation about this topic with a high school teacher revealed some interesting information. He was becoming increasingly frustrated with his students' low performance on classroom-based assessments. One of his students approached him during an extra help period and said, "I figured out a way to help [name omitted] with his homework during lunchtime. I think I can help other kids in the class if there is a way to do that."

Instead of feeling inadequate as a teacher, he took the opportunity to create a study hall in his classroom. After a few years of refining the process, he has acquired many strategies to help students teach others. He has seen an increase in performance, not only on classroom-based assessments but also on homework and standardized tests. He shared the following positive outcomes that he observed in his students after implementing strategies for teaching others:

- Encouraged higher-level thinking
- Enhanced active engagement and motivation
- Developed collaboration skills
- Decreased disruptive behavior
- Improved critical reflection skills
- Increased responsibility of student learning
- Focused instruction to student-centered instruction

Opportunities for Teaching Others

When you use whole-group instruction in your classroom, the same set of students may consistently raise their hands to share their answers, ideas, or observations. Rather than becoming frustrated, you could channel their leadership ability to teaching others.

In small-group work in a classroom, at least one student in a small group or pair may take the role of tutor while the other students take the role of the learner. Some students respond well in this scenario, as they are passive learners who are willing to let others do the work. However, this can be detrimental to learning. Students who may take longer to process information can feel deflated because their voices are not frequently heard. Observing different group dynamics can help you know when the time is right to employ teaching others.

Peer Teaching

This process requires the most thought and planning. Peer teaching works best when you have developed relationships with your students and created an environment in which they feel safe. As you think about using peer teaching, reflect on the following:

- How well do my students relate to each other at this point in the school year?
- Do my students know how to achieve our common goals?
- Are students showing evidence that they are learning the material?
- Am I already providing collaborative learning opportunities to allow the students to learn how to build and maintain collaborative relationships?
- Are the students open to learning new ways of learning?

Use the following guide to help you get started.

What to Do	Why Do It?
Observe students in small groups or pairs.	Identifies those students who feel comfortable in a lead role and those students who are in need of assistance.
Create new pairs or groups of students based on observations.	Employs the best-case scenarios for identifying qualified peer teachers.
Meet with students who are identified as peer teachers.	Provides an overview of what to do during a peer-teaching session, why it is important, and how it will help.
Determine the content areas and process skills you want students to learn and how they will be implemented.	Narrows the focus for the peer teachers so they do not feel overwhelmed.
Help peer teachers design the lessons/activities.	Provides peer teachers with materials and involves them as co-creators of the learning; provides a timeframe for the lesson.

Perhaps the most important aspect of starting the peer teaching process is helping peer teachers design the lessons/activities. Think about small-group activities that will not overwhelm the peer teacher.

Another important component of working with peer teachers is addressing non-content related issues:

- How can you gently correct students who are making mistakes without making them feel criticized or rejected?
- What are the best ways to provide positive feedback?
- What are the most effective ways to make all students in the group feel comfortable?

Examples of Peer Teaching Activities (All Content Areas and Grade Levels)

Games

One way to introduce students to the peer teaching strategy is to have the peer teacher play an educational game. This activity makes learning enjoyable and helps students feel more comfortable being taught by a peer. More information on games can be found in the chapter on games as a strategy. The following is an example from an elementary math class:

1. The peer teacher provides students with a three-column table labeled as follows: Numbers Rolled, Sum, Difference.

2. Students take turns rolling the dice. Depending on how many students are in the group and how much time is allotted, each student might be given the opportunity to take two or three turns.

3. For each pair of numbers, all students record the numbers rolled and write the correct equations for each sum and difference. The object of the game is to write as many correct equations as possible.

Numbers Rolled	Sum	Difference
1, 6	1 + 6 = 7 6 + 1 = 7	1 – 6 = –5 6 – 1 = 5
4, 3	4 + 3 = 7 3 + 4 = 7	4 – 3 = 1 3 – 4 = –1

4. The peer teacher records the correct answers each time the dice are rolled. After a specified number of rolls, the peer teacher reads all of the correct equations aloud. The group members submit the number of correct equations to the peer teacher and the winner(s) is crowned.

5. From this activity the peer teacher should have a good idea about who needs remediation or re-teaching. He or she should report observations to the classroom teacher and come up with new strategies for future lessons and activities.

Writing Round-Up

This technique is designed for students who have been given a writing assignment.

1. Explain to the group that Writing Round-Up is about sharing work with other students. Agree upon guidelines that students will use to review and edit each paper, such as staying neutral and providing timely and appropriate feedback in a positive manner. Remind students that this is a review and edit process and should not be nasty or hurtful.

2. Assign the peer teachers to one or two students and inform the peer teacher that he or she will act as the facilitator. Allow students ample time to review and edit.

3. Circulate around the room as students review and edit to ensure that the critiques are fair and objective.

4. Allow students to take home their assignments to polish them up before they turn them into you for a grade.

Presentations

Remind students that creating a presentation is one of the best ways to teach others. The following example is from a social studies class.

1. Give each group of students a topic to research and present to the class. For example, if the class is studying the Civil Rights Movement, students may research high-profile people such as Martin Luther King, Jr. Provide students with specific names or areas of interest.

2. Students research the topic and find pertinent information. They discuss and agree upon the best way to explain and present the information to other students. Encourage the use of technology and visual aids. In addition, encourage students to use resources other than their textbooks. Remind students that they will need to cite all of their sources.

3. Provide students with a deadline for submitting the first draft of their presentation. Decide whether their first draft needs corrections or suggestions. Give students time in the classroom to plan their presentation so that you can monitor their progress and provide specific and timely feedback.

4. On the day(s) of the presentations, set ground rules for respectful behavior. Give each group a specific amount of time for their presentation, and assign a student to be the timekeeper.

5. After each presentation, give students time to reflect. Build in time for a question-and-answer session and tell students to brainstorm ideas and questions for the group who presented.

Small Group Instruction

1. Give students an overview of a topic and provide each group with specific tasks. For example, give students the topic of the four seasons and ask them to come up with at least five questions about it. This brainstorming helps students learn from each other and also allows the teacher to assess prior knowledge. Students become more actively engaged in the learning process.

2. Assign one student to be the group reporter and have him or her share the group's ideas with the whole class. Assign another student to be the recorder for the whole class.

3. Discern if students are creating relevant questions or if they need to be guided in a more specific direction. After the whole-group sharing is done, ask students to return to their groups and do more in-depth research about the topic. Remind them that they can use a variety of resources.

4. Take the role of lead teacher and consolidate the information shared in the small groups. Use at least one idea from each group so that all students feel that they have made a contribution. Thank students for their hard work.

Peer Teaching: Strengths

Some strengths of peer teaching are as follows:

- Creates a rich cache of lessons to be used in the future
- Develops interpersonal and collaborative skills
- Facilitates a shared responsibility of teaching among students and the teacher
- Improves student confidence
- Improves retention skills and recall of information
- Provides students with ways to use their creativity
- Strengthens communication skills
- Strengthens problem-solving skills

Peer Teaching: Challenges

Some challenges of peer teaching are as follows:

- Individual learners might feel uncomfortable not having the "real" teacher facilitate the lessons and activities.

- Not all students who are initially identified as peer teachers turn out to be effective.
- Students might act more negatively because they do not receive direct consequences for negative behaviors from their peers.
- There might not be enough students who understand the content well enough to be considered a peer teacher.

Teaching Younger Students

Students who demonstrate a love of learning and a good command of a subject are good initial candidates for teaching younger students. Since many older students have younger brothers, sisters, or neighbors, most have some experience with being a teacher. When you decide to employ the strategy of teaching younger students, ask the selected students to reflect upon their knowledge of younger learners and their previous experience. The following are some guiding questions:

- With what age range of children have you worked?
- With what age range are you most comfortable?
- What subject do you think is most important to teach to younger learners? Why?
- What subject are you most comfortable teaching? Why? Describe how you would implement one lesson in this subject area.

Read through your students' responses and then have them write a description of younger students. If students have no experience directly working with younger children, ask them about friends, neighbors, or other relevant information they might possess. If students do have experience, ask them to identify the key characteristics they have observed. To help students learn compassion and empathy, ask students to reflect upon how they feel and what they think when they are in the position of learning something new. Remind them that these thoughts and feelings will be similar to the thoughts and feelings of the younger students.

What Skills Are Necessary to Help Younger Students Learn?

Older students have the charge of being the "expert other", so helping students prepare for teaching younger students should focus more on process skills than content knowledge. One such skill is communicating with younger students.

Younger students, especially those in primary grades, are particularly intuitive and can pick up on more non-verbal communication than most people realize. Guide your students to reflect on their communication styles, both verbal and non-verbal.

While the most successful students in your class may be obvious candidates for teaching younger students, remember that one result of teaching others is a deepened knowledge of the subject matter. Students who enjoy the challenge and opportunity to work with younger students often become more optimistic and confident students by growing in their knowledge of the subject matter and affirming how much they have learned. For example, a high school student who struggles with reading and lacks confidence may realize how much he or she does know when challenged to read with or to younger students. The student builds on proficiencies rather than focuses on deficiencies.

Another important skill for students to possess when working with younger learners is patience. Younger learners are typically more physically active and less able to concentrate for long periods of time. Students should create a learning opportunity that covers a variety of learning styles and has short, meaningful activities. Once you and your students make decisions about areas of content, keep in mind the following key ideas when creating lessons:

- Appropriately challenge students without being intimidating.
- Know the background knowledge of the students.
- Build on prior knowledge of the students.
- Be aware of the multi-sensory learning styles of the students.
- Make lessons fun and purposeful.
- Trade off active participation and listening. (When children become restless, be prepared to do something active.)

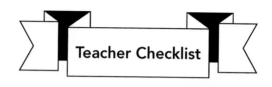

Teacher Checklist

Yes   No

☐   ☐   Students selected as peer teachers show evidence that they are learning the material.

☐   ☐   I already provide collaborative learning opportunities to allow the students to learn how to build and maintain collaborative relationships.

☐   ☐   Students show that they are open to learning different ways of learning.

☐   ☐   I identify those students who feel comfortable in a lead role and those students who are in need of more assistance.

☐   ☐   I consistently meet with students who are identified as peer teachers.

☐   ☐   I provide an overview of what it means to be a peer teacher — what to do during a peer teaching session, why it is important, and how it will help.

☐   ☐   I provide peer teachers with specific materials and involve them as co-creators of the learning.

☐   ☐   I provide a timeframe for each lesson and help peer teachers with time management of the session.

☐   ☐   Students demonstrate respectful behavior toward the peer teacher and each other.

☐   ☐   Students identified for teaching younger students submit a reflection about previous experience.

☐   ☐   Students show a positive attitude toward teaching others or teaching younger students.

KNOWLEDGE

APPLICATION

Test Preparation

Teacher Preparation for High-Stakes Assessments

Test taking is on the mind of every educator: "How do I get all of my students to perform so that they will pass the test? I am being evaluated on the performance of my students with this single event!" Educators need to teach well but also become test savvy in order to best prepare their students for annual high-stakes assessments. A high-stakes assessment refers to any state or national assessment that is used for accountability for students and/or schools. High-stakes tests are used for determining if students move to the next grade or graduate. They also determine if schools are ranked, awarded funding, or have sanctions invoked. The consequences are significant for staff and students.

- **Value the assessment.** Accept and recognize the purpose of the assessment. Students need to understand that working together throughout the entire school year will help them prepare. The time spent practicing testing strategies will directly affect the importance students place on the test. Only practicing the week before the test will not give the desired outcome.

- **Analyze the state assessment.** Know what content and standards are tested. Learn the test items, format of the test, and scoring of the test by researching the previous five years of assessment. Get a clear understanding of how the questions are written, the type of questions, the time allowed, and the various sections included on the assessment.

- **Determine what to teach by aligning your curriculum with the tested standards.** Become an expert at knowing what is tested and how students will be expected to demonstrate that knowledge.

Creating a Testing Environment

Creating a testing environment begins with the teacher. Have a positive attitude toward the assessment and help students feel relaxed when it is time for the assessment. To help students feel prepared, review aspects of the test: the format of the test, the timing of the various sections, the scoring, and the weighting of specific types of questions. Sharing this behind-the-scenes aspect of standardized tests will empower students by demystifying the tests and reducing the high anxiety often associated with them. The following are some helpful tips for creating a testing environment:

- Mirror the testing format in local assessments.

- Create test-taking tips posters to hang for easy reference, and refer to them throughout daily lessons.

- Clearly post the high-stakes test grading rubric around the classroom.

- Simulate the testing environment for students, especially if there will be movement in your school building. Students need to get used to who will be testing them in order to establish a rapport with that instructor.

- Create an interactive word wall with words students may likely come across on tests. Students need to use the words daily in order to become familiar with them, so choose a few words for the wall and rotate the words regularly.

Possible Testing Vocabulary Words for Word Walls	
accurate	main idea
article	mood
assumes	multiple meaning
author's purpose	occur
attitude	opinion
compare/contrast	organization(al)
conclude	passage
conflict	plot
draw conclusions	predicting
described	proofread
determine	prior knowledge
events	purpose
except	sentence structure
fiction	sequence
identify	setting
interpret	summarize

Reducing Test Anxiety for Students

Anxiety is often an emotional obstacle preventing students from showing their true level of knowledge and skill on a high-stakes test. Reduce student anxiety by having students do the following:

- Share their feelings of anxiety with parents and teachers.
- Think of the test as an opportunity to show what they know.
- Review homework and notes that pertain to the test topics.
- Try relaxation and breathing techniques to stay focused.
- Remember the test is only one way academic performance is measured.

Q-Card Strategy (Question-Card Strategy)

This strategy uses framed questions to familiarize both the teacher and student with the testing format of the questions. When a state establishes a pattern for the way it asks questions, this strategy is highly effective. Each assessment presents certain types of questions in a certain way, and creating question cards for students helps them become familiar with how the test addresses a particular skill. This works for both multiple choice and short/extended response questions. The following gives information about implementing the Q-card strategy:

- Visit the website for the high-stakes state or national test to seek information about how questions are formed. This is usually found in the item specifications section.

- Model each Q-card before allowing students to create their own questions based on the skill being asked of them.

- Have students create questions and exchange them with other students to practice answering questions.

Examples of Q-Cards

Identifying Author's Purpose Questions. Students are frequently asked to identify the author's purpose in a passage. This is a big picture type of question with which many students struggle. Students need to read and understand the entire passage in order to comprehend why the author wrote the passage, used specific words and phrases, or organized the passage in a specific format. Generally, an author's purpose is to entertain, persuade, inform, or establish an argument. Students should look for the following phrases in order to identify author's purpose questions.

- One of the main arguments is . . .
- The most accurate description for this article is . . .
- The best title for this article would be . . .
- This passage could best be summarized by . . .

Creating a Q-card with these question stems will assist students in identifying an author's purpose question on a reading test. If students can identify the skill being tested, they are more likely to answer the question correctly. In many cases, students are unaware of what they are being asked or what skill is being tested. Using Q-cards from the beginning of the school helps students become more confident in their test taking.

Finding the Main Idea. Main idea questions are one of the most common question types on standardized tests. Similar to author's purpose, main idea questions usually require students to comprehend the entire passage and identify an answer choice that best summarizes the plot, events, or argument presented in the passage. In order to identify the best main idea, students should base their answer solely on information presented in the passage. A main idea question may take one of the following forms:

- What is the main idea of . . . ?
- What is another good title for . . . ?
- Explain why the author probably titled the (article, story, poem).
- Write a summary of this (article, story, poem). Include only the most important information in the text.

Short/extended response questions may ask students to support their answers with relevant details, facts, statistics, or other information from the text.

Identifying Inference Questions. When students are asked to make an inference, they must interpret details from the passage. Inference questions may ask students to analyze or synthesize details in the story and can rarely be answered by an exact quote excerpted from the passage. Students must extend their knowledge and base their answer on details presented in the passage. An inference question may begin with the following:

- The author seems to feel that . . .
- The author refers to . . .

- The authors suggests that . . .
- The passage suggests . . .
- The author most likely means that . . .
- The author implies . . .

Drawing Conclusions About Information from the Text. A question that asks students to draw conclusions about information in the text may begin with the following:

- How does the author convey the meaning that . . . ?
- How does the author show . . . as (a) . . . ?
- What can the reader conclude after reading . . . ?
- What details, facts, or statistics led you to believe . . . ?
- Why does . . . act (behave) in this way (manner)?

Short/extended response questions may ask students to support their answers with relevant details, facts, statistics, or other information that supports the conclusions.

Tips on Answering Multiple-Choice Questions

Multiple-choice questions are the type most frequently asked on high-stakes tests. The following are suggestions for students on answering multiple-choice questions:

1. Skim the passage before you begin reading it.
   - Read the title.
   - Skim any subheadings, pictures, or graphs.
2. Read the questions carefully.
   - Look for important question words or phrases.
   - Use line or paragraph numbers if available.

3. Read the passage carefully.

 • Underline or circle important words or details.

 • Circle new or difficult words.

 • Take notes while reading.

4. Pick only one answer.

 • Read the question stem. Think of an answer in your head before looking at the possible answers. The choices given will not throw you off or trick you.

 • Find the answer choice that is most like your answer.

 • Mark only one answer. Sometimes two choices seem right. Consider the differences between the two answer choices. Sometimes one word can make the difference. Read the stem again then pick the right answer.

5. Make sure to answer every question.

 • Do not leave any blanks on the answer sheet.

 • If the question is too hard, then it is time to guess. Use the *process of elimination* to make your best guess.

Instruct students how to use the process of elimination to cross out answers:

1. Cross out answers that you know are wrong.

2. Use information only from the text. Cross out answers that are not found in the passage.

3. Make sure an answer is true.

4. Read the question stem again if needed and then make your best guess.

5. A positive choice is more likely to be true than a negative one.

Tips on Answering Short Answer/ Extended-Response Questions

Another popular form of questions is the short answer/extended-response questions. The following are suggestions for students on answering short answer/extended-response questions.

1. Do not leave these questions blank.
   - Show your work.
   - Write down your thoughts based on the text.
   - Even if you do not get the exact answer, partial credit is usually awarded.

2. If you do not know the answer, come back to it after you finish the rest of the test.
   - Be aware of the time you have left on the test.
   - Make an educated guess.
   - Remember that other parts of the test may give you clues about what the answer may be.

3. Read the question carefully and make sure that you answer all parts.
   - Most short/extended-response questions have multiple parts. In order to get full credit, all parts need to be answered in the space provided.
   - Look for question marks and words like *and* to count the number of tasks you are being asked to answer.

4. Short-answer questions usually require one or two sentences and about five minutes to complete.

5. Extended-response questions usually require more than one or two sentences and about 10 to 15 minutes to complete.

Tips for Answering Essay Questions

Essay questions are frequently the most challenging for students to answer and often have additional weighting that can greatly influence a student's overall score. The following are suggestions for answering essay questions:

1. Read the directions carefully. Pay close attention to whether you are supposed to answer all the essays or only a specified amount.

2. Make sure that you understand what the question is asking you.

3. Do not spend too much time on one essay question if you have more than one to answer.

4. If the question asks for facts, do not give your personal opinion on the topic.

5. When writing your essay, try to be as neat as possible.

6. Make an outline before writing your essay.

7. Do not write long introductions or conclusions. Your time should be spent on answering the question(s) being asked.

8. Focus on one main idea per paragraph.

9. If you have time left at the end, proofread your work and correct any errors.

10. If you make a mistake, simply draw a line through it. It is much neater and quicker than erasing it.

Tips for Solving Math Word Problems

Learning how to solve problems in mathematics requires knowing what to look for. Math problems often require established procedures and knowing when to apply them. To identify what to do, be familiar with what the problem is asking. You must identify the given information, find an appropriate strategy, and utilize the information within the problem to come up with a reasonable solution.

Problem solving requires practice. The more practice you give your students, the better they become.

Problem Solving Plan in Four Steps

1. **Clues**
   - Read the problem carefully.
   - Underline clue words.
   - Ask yourself if you have seen a problem similar to this one. If so, what do you recognize? What did you need to do?
   - What facts are you given?
   - What do you need to find out?

2. **Game Plan**
   - What is your plan of action?
   - Have you seen a problem like this before? Identify what you did.
   - Define your strategies to solve this problem.
   - Try out your strategies (using formulas, simplifying, using sketches, guess and check, looking for a pattern).
   - Try something. Remember there are only four operations that you can use: addition, subtraction, multiplication, or division.

3. **Solve**
   - Use your strategies to solve the problem.

4. **Reflect**
   - Look over your solution.
   - Does it seem reasonable?
   - Did you answer the question?
   - Did you answer using the language and/or units as the question?

Analyzing Past Tests

This strategy can be very effective using either classroom or standardized tests. It allows the students to analyze why they may have chosen the wrong choice. Teachers can make a chart to assist students in identifying any patterns in their wrong choices.

Class: _____

Date of exam: _____

Grade: _____

How did you study for this test? (time spent, strategies used, etc.)

Questions Missed

Question # _____:

Write out entire question:

Points Lost _____

Type of question _____

Why did you miss this question? (carelessness, no knowledge of content, misunderstood question, didn't finish)

---

1. Under Questions Missed, write in the numbers of the actual test questions that were incorrect on your test. If you missed questions 4, 8, 13, and 27, those are the numbers you should write in that blank.

2. For example, if you got #4 wrong, determine the following:
   - How many points were taken off?
   - What kind of question or problem was it?
   - What do you think was the reason that you got it wrong?

3. Look for patterns. Ask the following:
   - What kinds of questions did you have the most difficulty with?
   - Which questions were worth the most points?

- What can you do to improve on your next test?
- How can you make sure you get more of the high-value questions correct next time?

4. Make a list of the things that you need to do to be more successful on your next test. Ask the following questions:

- How can I make sure I understand the material?
- Do I need to manage my time better so I can spend more time studying?
- How can I determine what is important to study?
- How should I prepare for the test?
- What strategies should I use while taking the test?
- What did I learn from my successes and failures?

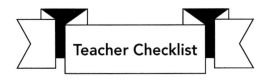

Teacher Checklist

Yes   No

☐   ☐   Assessments are positively valued in discussions and actions.

☐   ☐   Ample time is allotted to prepare for the assessment.

☐   ☐   Past assessments are analyzed in each content area.

☐   ☐   Curriculum is aligned with the tested standards.

☐   ☐   Testing rubrics are posted in the classroom.

☐   ☐   An interactive word wall with the testing vocabulary is used.

☐   ☐   Opportunities are provided for students to talk about how they are feeling toward the assessment.

☐   ☐   Students are assisted with realizing the purpose of what is being tested.

☐   ☐   Students learn coping techniques for stress.

☐   ☐   Question stems similar to the assessment are used in the classroom.

☐   ☐   Suggestions on how to tackle each question type are posted in the classroom.

☐   ☐   A variety of questions are created for classroom assessments that mirror the high-stakes assessment.

☐   ☐   Students are provided opportunities to review classroom assessments after the test.

K
N
O
W
L
E
D
G
E

APPLICATION

Video

Video as a Strategy

Learning frequently requires acquiring new information and ideas. Video is an effective instructional strategy for introducing content to students. At one time, video was expensive and offered limited content and accessibility. Often a teacher had to plan ahead to schedule equipment and obtain a copy of the video. With the explosion in computer and Internet tools, it is now very easy and cost effective to record, edit, and display video in the classroom.

Students are very comfortable with video and often prefer it to written text or oral presentations. Teachers can use this student interest to their advantage in crafting engaging and relevant lessons. Video helps students retain more information, understand concepts more rapidly, and develop enthusiasm about learning topics. Using video as one component in a thoughtful lesson plan, students can make new connections among curriculum topics and discover links between these topics and the world. When video is combined with other strategies, the teacher can create powerful learning experiences. For example, short video clips can be used to build background knowledge prior to students reading a required piece of text, or students may watch a video and write to reflect on information acquired in the video.

Video is uniquely suited to do the following:

- Take students on impossible field trips (for example, inside the human body or off to other planets)
- Take students around the world to meet new people and hear their ideas
- Illustrate complex, abstract concepts through animated, 3-D images
- Show experiments that cannot be done in class
- Enhance great literature, plays, or music
- Bring to life important scenes from history

Effective use of video can help teachers do the following:

- Reach students with a variety of learning styles (especially visual learners) and information acquisition styles
- Engage students in problem solving and investigative activities
- Begin to dismantle social stereotypes through introduction of different cultures
- Help students practice media literacy and critical viewing skills
- Provide a common experience for students to discuss critical issues such as protecting the environment or reducing poverty

Using Video

Video should not be considered a substitute for good instruction any more than watching television in the home is a substitute for parental supervision of children. Video can be very engaging, but it also needs to be educational. Teachers can achieve both engagement value and education value by carefully planning the use of video in the classroom.

Planning Before Instruction

- Preview the video to make sure it is appropriate and useful and assess the value of the program's support materials.

- Select segments that are most relevant to the curricular focus of the day. A brief video clip can spark student interest or demonstrate a concept and is often more effective than showing a full length movie. Showing a particular segment conserves valuable classroom time and focuses the lesson for students. Use students' time efficiently, and do not show extraneous portions of the video.

- Prepare the classroom for viewing by checking equipment (monitor, video player, Internet, audio, remote control) and arranging seating and lighting. Lights should be left on as much as possible to reinforce that video is not passive entertainment.

Preparing Students Before Instruction

Do not simply show a video. Prepare students to watch a video and look for specific information that relates to the intended learning.

- Ask students thought-provoking questions.
- Explain why the video is being used.
- Prepare students for important visual images.
- Discuss major points covered by the program.
- Provide focus activities or viewing directions for individuals, small groups, or the entire class.
- Present new vocabulary and/or review material necessary for understanding program content.
- List key concepts on the board or computer display.
- Conduct a related hands-on activity.
- Have students look for specific events or follow certain characters in the video.
- Use a form or graphic organizer for students to record observations. This keeps students on task and directs the learning experience toward the lesson's objectives.

During Instruction

- Use the pause button effectively to enhance the viewing experience. You might pause to do the following:
  - Control the pace and amount of information.
  - Check for student comprehension.
  - Solicit inferences and make predictions.
  - Define a word in context.
  - Highlight a point.
  - Ask students to make connections to other topics or real-world events.
  - Change the pace by asking students to come up and point to something on the screen, write in journals, or replicate what they have seen.
  - Replay and review important portions of the video, especially if students have missed a point.
- As an option, eliminate the sound from a video segment. When you eliminate sound, you can use any video to instruct at almost any grade level, using your own age-appropriate narration. You can also ask students to describe and comment on what they see which is an excellent technique for assessing students' prior knowledge or reviewing and evaluating what they have learned.
- Encourage media literacy by helping students recognize elements of video production, such as camera angles, music, shot composition, and the role of the actors. Students can evaluate a video's effectiveness and discuss the ways that audiences might be manipulated or influenced by choices made during production.

After Instruction

Students should feel that the video is an integral part of their learning experience, so teachers need to follow up the video with culminating hands-on activities, student-centered projects, and student- or teacher-designed investigations. Ideally, video is used in conjunction with a variety of activities that make an expansive, hands-on learning experience: field trips, guest speakers, letter writing projects, and journal writing.

Options for Accessing Video

Several options are available for accessing video in the classroom. Not all options are available in every school. Each option offers advantages and disadvantages as well as differing costs.

Streaming Internet Site — Public

Thousands of videos are on the Internet now. These range from gigantic video aggregators, such as YouTube, to schools and not-for-profit education groups that post video.

Advantages

- Generally costs nothing to access

Disadvantages

- Requires some planning time to find, review, and record location of video
- Requires Internet connection to play video
- Often has low quality video
- May experience speed issues due to slow Internet access
- May be limited or denied by filtering systems
- Could disappear at any time

Streaming Internet Site — Subscription

Many education and commercial sources provide educational videos that require schools or districts to use an access password. These range from textbook publishers that provide supplemental videos to organizations that provide education videos as a purchased school service.

Advantages

- Has high quality video

Disadvantages

- Requires Internet connection to play video
- Requires password
- Costs money for subscription

Stored on Local Network Server

School districts can avoid limitations of Internet by creating an internal network-based video server. This might include purchased or licensed video clips. All computers on the local network would have access to all district videos.

Advantages
- Available to all teachers
- Not limited by Internet or filtering system

Disadvantages
- Costs money for set up and maintenance
- Limits teacher to videos licensed by the district
- Can be difficult or expensive to add new videos

Stored Copy on Local Computer

The best way to guarantee access to video is to have a copy locally stored on a computer in the classroom. You can accomplish this in several ways: copy a DVD to a digital form on the computer; convert an audio tape to digital form and save on a computer; copy an Internet-based video to your local computer. These activities require specialized software that is sometimes free and other times may have additional costs. You also have to be aware of copyright laws in making any copies.

Copying videos ensures that you will have access to the video and also makes editing a longer video to an instructionally important clip easier. Only a decade ago video editing was a complicated task requiring thousands of dollars of dedicated equipment. Today, specialized video editing software makes this a doable task on most computers. Editing helps to make video convenient but also requires time to learn editing software and prepare the video.

Advantages
- Provides consistently available video
- Can hold larger, reliable movie files (with better resolution)

- Easier to control, allowing teacher to show only a portion, pause, or skip over portions
- Easy to set up for students to watch again or to watch if they missed a class

Disadvantages
- May require additional software to copy and edit video
- May be prohibited by copyright and software restrictions
- May require screen capture of many web movies that are not directly downloadable/savable

Stored Copy on Portable Device

This option uses small portable devices such as the *Apple iPod*. You can store multiple videos on these devices, and they can be even more convenient than a local computer. You can easily review videos on your portable device or connect the device to a projector to show video to the class. Students could also view video individually and at a later time directly from a portable device.

Advantages
- Convenient to move videos to any location
- Allows students to view video on their own devices

Disadvantages
- Requires time to convert videos
- Costs money for devices

Stand Alone DVD

Purchased videos are usually placed in digital format on DVDs and historically in analog format on videotape. You can retain these videos in this format and use the DVD or tape each time you present them.

Advantages
- Little preparation time required

Disadvantages

- Requires physical storage space
- Can get lost or damaged
- Requires another device to play videos
- May be hard to show just a portion of the video

Legal Aspects

Copyright laws protect rights of video creators, and teachers must be careful to follow and respect these provisions of the law. Since it has become very easy to duplicate video, teachers and students can easily cross the line of legal activity. While there is little chance that teachers will be cited for illegal copies, teachers should follow legal and ethical provisions of copyright. This begins with understanding the law and exemptions. Teachers also are role models for students and should inform them about copyright laws regarding video.

While copyright laws prohibit the unauthorized duplication and presentation of video materials, some provisions in the law allow educators "fair use" for educational purposes. *Fair use* is the right, in some circumstances, to quote or duplicate copyrighted material without asking permission or paying for it.

- Fair use applies to copyrighted videos that are legitimately acquired (a legal copy). They must be used in a classroom or similar place "dedicated to face-to-face instruction," not for use as entertainment or reward. Teachers may use copyrighted materials in the classroom without restrictions of length, percentage, or multiple uses.

- If replacements are unavailable at a fair price or are available only in obsolete formats, videos may be copied for archival purposes or to replace lost, damaged, or stolen copies.

Video Sources

The following are several sources for locating video for classroom use in many subject areas and grade levels.

Commercial Sources

Discovery Education — http://discoveryeducation.com

Disney Educational Productions — http://dep.disney.go.com

BrainPop — www.brainpop.com

NBC Learn — www.nbclearn.com

Not-for-Profit Sources

Cable in the Classroom — www.ciconline.org

NASA — www.nasa.gov

Free Internet Sites

5 Min Videopedia — www.5min.com

Academic Earth — http://academicearth.org

Annenberg Media — www.learner.org

Brightstorm — www.brightstorm.com

CosmoLearning — www.cosmolearning.com

Edublogs.tv — www.edublogs.tv

Futures Channel — www.thefutureschannel.com

How Stuff Works — www.howstuffworks.com

Hulu — http://www.hulu.com

Ibiblio — http://ibiblio.org

Internet Archive — www.archive.org/details/movies

iTunesU — www.apple.com/education/itunes-u

Khan Academy — www.khanacademy.org

MIT World — http://mitworld.mit.edu

NeoK12 — www.neok12.com

PBS — http://video.pbs.org

Regents Review Live — www.regentsreviewlive.net

ResearchChannel — www.youtube.com/ResearchChannel

SchoolTube — www.schooltube.com

Sqooltube — http://sqooltube.com

ScienceStage — http://sciencestage.com

Teacher TV — www.teachers.tv

TeacherTube — www.teachertube.com

TED (Technology, Entertainment, Design) — www.ted.com

WatchKnow.org — www.watchknow.org

YouTube EDU — www.youtube.com/edu

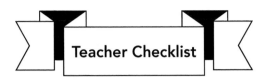

Teacher Checklist

Yes   No

☐   ☐   Videos relate to instructional objectives.

☐   ☐   Only the portion of the video that is relevant to learning is shown.

☐   ☐   Videos are obtained legally.

☐   ☐   Purpose of watching the video is clear to students.

☐   ☐   Students are given assignments of things to watch for, reflect on, or record during the video.

☐   ☐   Video equipment is checked in advance of class presentation to ensure proper operation.

☐   ☐   Equipment works well to provide video that can be seen and heard properly.

☐   ☐   Video is good quality for students to easily see desired content and hear audio.

☐   ☐   Videos are properly stored or referenced for future use.

☐   ☐   Students have access to replay video for lesson review, individual work, or independent study.

APPLICATION

Writing to Learn

Making Meaning Through Informal Writing

Writing-to-learn activities are *informal* writing assignments that ask students to think through the concepts on which they are working. It provides order to their thoughts and shapes meaning out of new ideas and notions. Students are asked to think logically and encouraged to personalize their learning at that moment.

Writing to learn is a thinking-and-learning technique that develops and improves the quality of student writing. Writing-to-learn strategies are varied and have many formats. Usually, these writing tasks are short and appealing. They energize students and encourage new thinking. The following are several examples:

- Teachers begin the class with five minutes of student writing on yesterday's lecture or readings.
- To check for learning, teachers stop the lecture for a quick write about the meaning of their preceding statement.

- At the end of a lab, science teachers ask students to give a five-minute recap on what transpired during the experiment, what worked, and what went wrong.
- Students in math write a quick process explanation on solving the new equation.
- Social studies students write their thoughts and beliefs on the First Amendment while discussing the Bill of Rights.

Central to all this writing is its freedom, lack of form, personal audience, and engagement of the writer's mind.

The traditional process of writing a paper on an academic topic typically includes the five steps of pre-writing, drafting, revising, editing, and publishing. When students learn to write, they use an analytic thinking process with an emphasis on the revision stage, and generally, the format is an essay, a longer report, or a research paper. When students write to learn, they use a broader thinking process. The emphasis is on making connections with course content and discovering new understandings. Writing-to-learn formats include journal entries, short notes, and commentary. Students write to explore, personalize, and become more familiar with course content.

Writing to Learn	Learning to Write
journals and learning logs	book reports
lab logs and notebooks	research reports
quick writes	essays
short narratives	lab reports
summaries	opinion editorials
dialogues	technical writing

Why Writing Is Important

- Writing allows students an opportunity to deepen their thoughts and make critical mental connections between thought and concrete content. It forces them to slow down their thinking and to carefully analyze material.

- Writing increases retention of information because it forces the learner to take time to carefully analyze the subject matter.

- Writing to learn provides teachers with an effective way to assess the understanding of all learners while helping students focus on critical thinking.

- Writing to learn provides students an opportunity to actively engage with course content. Students who write in response to material learned begin to do the following:
  - Think independently
  - Develop insight
  - Explore thoughts and feelings
  - Develop intellectual courage
  - Reason logically
  - Follow the thread of the lesson in their minds
  - Visualize a concept and then make it more concrete

Strategies for Writing to Learn

The following are several generic writing strategies that can easily be adapted to most subjects and grade levels. Think of ways to keep your students writing, even if it is not a formal graded essay.

Free Writing

Free writing is an unstructured form of writing which allows students to write "freely," without consideration of grammar, sentence structure, or technique. Free writing is an instructional strategy used for a set period of time. It allows students to generate thoughts regarding a certain topic and can be used before or after teaching a concept.

To use before teaching a concept:

- Give students a predetermined amount of time (typically 3, 5 or 10 minutes).
- Ask students to write everything they know regarding a topic.
- Encourage students to write as quickly as possible, ignoring any mistakes they make in their writing.
- If students cannot think of anything to write, they write that they can't think of anything until a thought occurs.

When used before teaching a concept, free writing allows a teacher to understand what students know and do not know about certain content.

Double-Entry Journals

In double-entry journals, students sharpen study, reading comprehension, critical thinking, and analysis skills. Students begin by dividing a notebook sheet down the center with a vertical line. On the left side, they write notes from the lecture, lines from the text, or course content facts. These need not be written exactly; students can condense the material to include the main ideas. Alternatively, they can write a summary of the facts and information as long as they maintain the meaning of the original text.

Next, students fill in the right side with their comments and reactions to the notes on the left. This format of journal entry organizes students' notes and keeps valuable information separated on the left side. The students interact with the text when they fill in the right side of the page. Teachers can model the process and then brainstorm with students about ways to respond. Teachers can also help students develop the right-side writing skill by asking them to compare ideas, make comments, list their personal connections with the information, analyze, or ask questions. Ideas for right-side journal entries include the following:

- Explanation of confusing lines of text
- Questions about parts of the content that they do not understand
- Comments about whether they agree or disagree with the author and why

- Paraphrased version of the left-side text
- Diagrams or drawings that interpret the text
- Comparisons to information students recall from earlier course content
- Associations with information from other courses
- Extensions of the information based on personal experience
- Effects of this information on the world outside the classroom

Thinking Cubes

Thinking cubes are used to expose students to a variety of higher order thinking questions. Teachers prepare a cube with a recall, analysis, synthesis, or evaluation question on each side of the cube.

Students work in groups to roll the cube and answer the question on which it lands. After discussing the answer, they record their group's answer in their daily journals. (Wormeli)

Inside/Outside Circles

Inside/outside circles give students a chance to hear the thinking of others and respond to them. To complete this activity, students need to be placed in an inner or outer circle. Start by dividing the class in half. The first half forms a large circle and faces toward the center of the circle. The second half stands inside the first circle and faces a partner on the outside circle. Students should be close enough to have a conversation. Ask the inner circle to ask their partner to respond to a review question about something recently learned. Some examples of questions may be as follows:

- Do you agree with the author of the text? Why or why not?
- What do you think is the most important part of the text we just read?
- Can you think of a better solution than the one we just learned about?
- What would be different today if the event we just learned about did not occur?

Give students a minute or less to respond to the question. As the students in the outer circle give their answer, the inner circle writes notes about that conversation. Then the outer circle writes notes regarding how the inner circle responded. Once a minute has passed, the outer circle moves a particular number of students clockwise while the inner circle stays still. Students are asked to repeat the question and continue to write notes. Once the students have asked the question of several partners, the question can be changed.

Narratives

Another tool used to capture students' thoughts or focus them on the material is the narrative. By tapping into their personal experiences, students build bridges from their lives to the concept they are studying. In relating to the material being taught, students write a narrative about something that has happened to them, something they have read about, an event in a relative's life, or a story they remember. This helps build relevance of curriculum in students' minds.

The following are examples of connecting narrative threads to course content for the day:

- Teachers can set up a narrative in a science class by asking students to write a quick narrative on viruses they have contracted.

- In a history or literature class, students can write a narrative in the words of a character or national hero, such as Paul Revere's thoughts as he prepared for his famous ride.

- In a technology class, students can write a short history of their personal involvement with computers.

- Students can write a narrative about a friend or relative who has undergone circumstances similar to those being studied in a class.

A narrative is a personalized way to get students to link course content to their lives. Often, teachers ask students to share their narratives in small groups to start discussions on the significance and value of their experiences. These narrative links become the basis for a depth of learning and greater understanding of the material being presented.

Directed Reading/Thinking Activity (DR/TA)

In the directed reading/thinking activity, students divide their papers into four sections and respond to four statements — "What I know I know," "What I think I know," "What I think I'll learn," and "What I know I learned" — to practice comprehension and retention of information. In this strategy, students activate their prior knowledge to connect with new information. In the first three sections of the DR/TA sheet, students use brainstorming skills to "download" the information they know, think they know, and expect to learn about a specific topic. Since students are not graded on the correctness of their answers, this method is risk free. Students write and think freely without penalty. Finally, the last section of the sheet, "What I know I learned," allows students to compare and connect their prior knowledge with new information they have just learned.

What I know I know:
What I think I know:
What I think I'll learn:
What I know I learned:

Jigsaws

This technique allows students an opportunity to research a large topic without becoming overwhelmed with that topic. This collaborative technique allows each student an opportunity to be a teacher and leader within the group. It can be used over a period of days or within one class while trying to read a section of the textbook.

Students are divided into small groups and given a topic to study. All groups can study the same topic, or different topics can be given to each group. Students are asked to take a large topic and break it into smaller parts. (This may be done with the guidance of the teacher). Each student then researches his or her part of the topic, writes a summary of the research and shares that summary with the group members. After all group members have had an opportunity to write their summary, they share that summary with other groups.

Summaries

To aid student comprehension of the material, teachers may stop the lesson at any point and ask students to write a summary of what they understand so far. Alternatively, they might ask students to read the text and respond in a short statement that summarizes the main points. This writing-to-learn technique focuses students' commentaries on an overview of their understanding at that point in time. Through summary, students review the materials and record what they have absorbed in synopsis form.

Determining whether students understand the content is important before moving ahead in the lesson. Summaries give teachers an opportunity to know how much students grasp and whether review is necessary before adding additional information. Summaries are sometimes read aloud in small groups or as a class. Just the act of reading aloud gives students an oral review that involves auditory learning. Teachers gauge student comprehension and determine points that need review and re-teaching. More on summarization is included in this handbook.

RAFT

RAFT stands for **role** (of the writer), **audience, format,** and **topic**. The RAFT strategy is a post-reading activity designed to demonstrate student understanding of the material in a creative and relevant way. Students enjoy stepping out of the traditional academic role and assuming a professional role as a writer and problem solver. RAFT exercises are effective as performance assessments at the end of a unit. Students should apply the information they learned from their reading to their new audience and purpose.

After students have read text on a specific topic, they are placed in the role of someone in the professional world who would use the information on the job. For example, you might connect their studies on the auditory system to nurses' aides, doctors, hearing aid manufacturers, new parents, technology innovators, and others. To develop a RAFT assignment, use the following steps:

- **Role**: After reading, ask students to take the role of someone in the professional world.

- **Audience**: Give students an audience. Who needs the information they just learned in class? For instance, when students finish the auditory system unit, tell them their role is an aide in a pediatric office. The doctor wants them to help parents (the audience) better understand ear infections in their young children.

- **Format**: Determine what product the students are going to develop, design, or present. You can also ask for student input on the most effective formats for the task at hand. The format should apply in the role they are assuming. In the role of a doctor's aide, an academic report would not be typical of the workplace situation; however, a brochure would be an appropriate format since the doctor could give it to parents when their children contract ear infections.

- **Topic**: The topic is determined by the unit of study. In this case, the topic is infections in the ear. Students will use the information they learned in the unit. In addition, they will need to take the topic one step further by researching infections of the ear.

For younger students or in a more creative context, you might brainstorm imaginary situations where students can demonstrate an understanding of the material. For example, "A tiny cave explorer enters the ear canal and writes about her encounters in her exploration log."

Ideas for Student Products/Formats
- Outline plans for a half-day workshop.
- Create a citywide program and write an action plan.
- Design a brochure.

- Design a performance review form.
- Write an action plan.
- Develop a proposal.
- Design a flyer with a mail back portion.
- Write a corporate philosophy.
- Write an employee handbook section with guidelines.
- Write a letter of recommendation.
- Design and conduct a survey.
- Prepare a multimedia presentation.

Quick Writes

Quick writes are short writing exercises that can be used at the beginning, during, or end of a lesson. The following are prompts for typical quick write activities.

To Begin Instruction

- What do you already know about this?
- What questions do you have from your reading?
- Write one key point from yesterday's lesson.
- What is something important for you to know about this topic?

During Instruction

- What do you think about this information?
- How is this like . . . ?
- What is a significant question you would ask? Why?
- What do you think will happen next?
- Identify a potential problem or issue.

After Instruction

- What is something important you learned today?
- What do you think are the two most important points?

- Write three things you would say to explain this to a younger child (or adult).
- What did you do to participate today?
- What would you like to know more about?
- What did you enjoy and/or not enjoy about this discussion?
- What is something you are doing to help yourself learn?
- What is something you have accomplished since we began this topic?
- What do you think about this idea/topic?
- What do you not understand?
- How could you use this to . . . ?

References

Wormeli, R. *Summarization in any subject: 50 techniques to improve student learning*. Alexandria, VA: Association of Supervision and Curriculum Development, 2005.

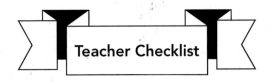

Teacher Checklist

Yes No

☐ ☐ Students are given notice of expectations for writing prior to introducing the information.

☐ ☐ Students are given the opportunity to respond to the material they have learned.

☐ ☐ Students are encouraged to avoid rote recall of information and focus on analyzing, synthesizing, and evaluating the learned material.

☐ ☐ Students are given a basic structure for writing.

☐ ☐ All students practice various writing-to-learn techniques.

☐ ☐ Students are encouraged to keep thoughts concise.

☐ ☐ Students are encouraged to express and form their own thoughts around the material they have been taught.

☐ ☐ Students are reminded that there is often not a single right answer.

☐ ☐ Students are given positive feedback on effective parts of their writing.

☐ ☐ Forms and graphic organizers are sometimes used to guide and record student thoughts.

☐ ☐ Frequent quick writes are used to check student understanding.